The Complete
Trailer Handbook

The Complete
Trailer Handbook

Richard Newton

First published in 2008 by Motorbooks, an imprint of MBI Publishing Company, 400 First Avenue North, Suite 300, Minneapolis, MN 55401 USA

Motorbooks titles are also available at discounts in bulk quantity for industrial or sales-promotional use. For details write to Special Sales Manager at MBI Publishing Company, 400 First Avenue North, Suite 300, Minneapolis, MN 55401 USA.

To find out more about our books, join us online at www.motorbooks.com.

Library of Congress Cataloging-in-Publication Data

Newton, Richard, 1944–
    The complete trailer handbook / Richard Newton.
        p. cm.
    Includes bibliographical references and index.
    ISBN 978-0-7603-3371-6 (sb : alk. paper)
    1. Automobile trailers—Handbooks, manuals, etc. I. Title.
    TL297.N47 2008
    688.6—dc22
                                              2008010233

On the cover: Whether for work or hobbies, there is a trailer for just about every purpose.

Top left, bottom left: *Featherlite Trailers*

Top right, bottom right: *Wells-Cargo, Inc.*

On the title page: The various purposeful modifications to this trailer highlight the owner's ingenuity.

On the back cover: The ever-popular aluminum-bodied utility trailer.

About the Author

Richard Newton is an ASE Master Technician who spent 15 years in the auto service industry before becoming a magazine editor and freelance automotive writer. His Motorbooks titles include *Wheel and Tire Performance Handbook, Ultimate Garage Handbook, Autocross Performance Handbook, Corvette C5 Performance Projects 1997–2004, 101 Projects for Your Corvette 1984–1996, How to Restore and Modify Your Corvette 1968–1982, and Corvette Restoration Guide 1963–1967.*

Designer: Diana Boger

Printed in Singapore

CONTENTS

CHAPTER 1
TYPES OF TRAILERS

The word "trailer" can be used to describe any type of rolling platform that has a hitch and some wheels. All trailers can be towed by something, and all trailers have wheels. Trailers can be grouped into several basic categories: utility trailers, horse trailers, boat trailers, motorcycle trailers, Jet Ski trailers, snowmobile trailers, and travel trailers. Within each category, there may be hundreds of variations.

UTILITY TRAILERS

Forget about horse trailers, enclosed race car haulers, and other purpose-specific trailers; the utility trailer is where the real action is. This is the trailer you take to the home improvement store to pick up a bunch of bricks to create a walking path in your garden or wood for that huge deck you're building off the back of your house.

Utility trailers comprise a wide variety of trailers, and because of this the term "utility trailer" is difficult to define. Most of the time, a utility trailer is a single-axle trailer that can carry up to 2,000 pounds. Some utility trailers have sides and some do not. Some even have sides that are removable. No matter how it's configured, the utility trailer is a basic all-purpose trailer for household chores.

It's easier to define what a utility trailer is not. A utility trailer is not a single-purpose trailer. Horse trailers and boat trailers can only do one thing: haul horses or boats. Utility trailers can do a number of things. The less you intend to haul with your trailer, the smaller it can be. However, when purchasing a utility trailer, you should think about buying a trailer slightly bigger than you think you need. Who knows what you'll want to haul next month?

HORSE TRAILERS

Horses are big and heavy and require a dedicated, purpose-built trailer. I think hauling a horse may be more difficult than hauling a race car. Unlike boats, snowmobiles, and race cars, horses are living, breathing animals. There are two basic choices in horse trailers: tag-alongs, which hook to the rear of a truck, or goosenecks, which attach to the bed of a pickup.

A few people still refer to tag-along trailers as "bumper hitch trailers," although these days only a tiny trailer can connect solely to a bumper since most bumpers are now made of high-tech plastic instead of something stronger like steel. Most tag-along trailers require a hitch that mounts to a vehicle frame.

Many horse owners choose to purchase a gooseneck trailer because it offers a couple of advantages over the tag-along trailer, the most important of which is its stability. Having the trailer's tongue weight over the rear axle of your truck improves handling, so you enjoy a smoother, more stable ride.

Even a basic trailer like this one has tires, wheel bearings, and a lighting system—all of which will require your attention at one point or another.

Because the gooseneck hitch connects in the bed of the truck, the overall length of the rig is shorter than that of a tag-along trailer with equivalent floor space. Most people also find that gooseneck hitches are easier to hitch and unhitch than a frame hitch, due to improved visibility of the hitch and king pin while aligning truck and trailer.

The advantage of a tag-along trailer, besides the cheaper price, is the ability to tow the trailer with something other than a pickup truck. Tag-alongs are also smaller than gooseneck trailers, which means they're easier to haul and easier to store when not in use. If you don't need additional space for sleeping or storage, the extra expense for a gooseneck trailer may not be necessary.

When selecting a horse trailer, remember that horses are claustrophobic by nature. The more room, light, and ventilation there is in the trailer, the happier your horse will be. In practical terms, this means that the horse will travel more comfortably, load more easily, and be less likely to injure itself. Better travel accommodations will also make your horse less likely to suffer from stress problems. Bottom line: Your horse will be much happier in a comfortable, spacious trailer, and a happy horse will make you happier.

No matter which style of trailer you prefer, the size of the horse is an important factor. The horse should have enough room to move its legs forward and sideways to keep its balance while the trailer is moving. Narrow trailers and trailers with full center dividers can cause a horse to scramble if it can't spread its legs enough to keep its balance.

Thankfully, nearly all newer horse trailers are equipped with rubber torsion suspensions. Give this feature serious consideration when choosing horse transportation. Torsion suspension reduces the amount of shock the horse absorbs through the floor of the trailer, thereby reducing stress on the horse. This type of suspension also brings with it a safety advantage: If a tire on the trailer goes flat while in use, the remaining three wheels will carry the trailer until you can get to a safe place to change the tire.

When looking at a horse trailer to purchase, check to make sure there are no sharp edges anywhere on the trailer, inside or out, so your horse will not be inadvertently injured. Horses can also trip on floorboards, so make sure the trailer's floorboards run the length of the trailer rather than across the trailer. There should also be good support underneath the floor. Remember: Because a horse has four legs, the weight of the horse is going to be concentrated on four points inside the trailer.

After you've considered your horse's needs, you can consider your own. Will you be hauling your horse long distances, or *continued on page 12*

This custom trailer is simply loaded with nice features. Check out how the lighting is protected. Also note the special rack for the gas can.

This trailer is properly connected for towing. Note how it is parallel to the ground. Placing the load on the trailer properly can make a huge difference in how the trailer pulls down the road.

This car hauler has a raised front, which can keep rocks and stones from hitting the car you are hauling. The triangular shape to the front might provide minor aerodynamic benefits as well. Notice how this owner has created a storage compartment in the front, directly behind the spare tire.

Landscape trailers like this one are usually perfect for fulfilling the average suburban homeowner's hauling needs. This rig will haul mulch, equipment, supplies, and just about anything else you might need. Because it is small and lightweight, you can just pick it up by the tongue and move it around when you're not using it.

Notice the white strip on the trailer right below the car's left rear wheel. By lining up the car's rear wheel with this line, the owner knows that he will get the weight of the load balanced properly. This owner may not be into aesthetics, but he obviously pays attention to loading.

This is a very versatile trailer. All of the sides can be removed, as well as the rear ramp, giving this model the flexibility to haul longer items.

The owner of this Corvette made a specialized trailer for hauling tires to autocross events. He also added a second storage compartment in front of the main box. I give him points for the creative spare tire mount.

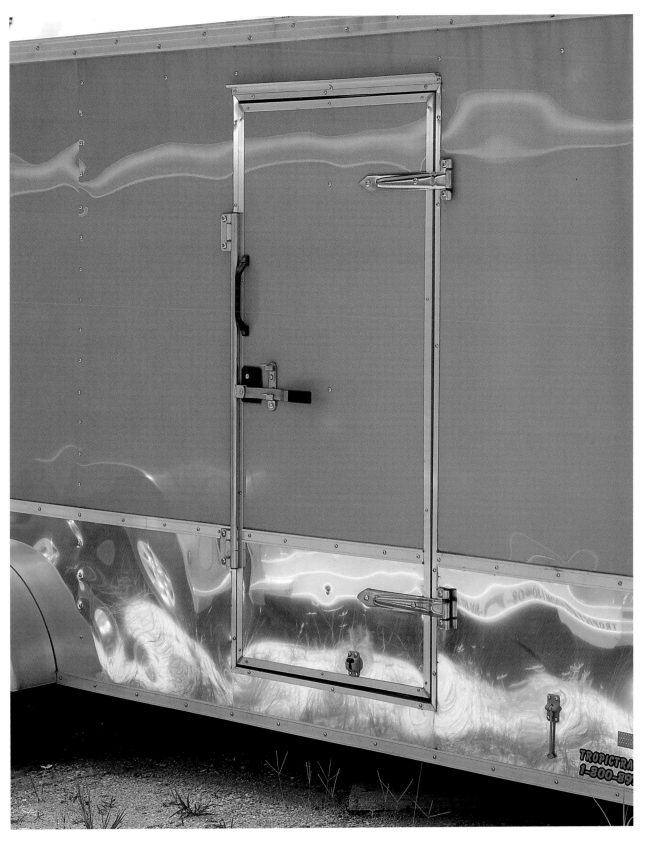

The door hinges on this enclosed trailer are more than adequate. Too often a manufacturer will cut corners on hardware to meet a price point and, after a few years, the doors start to sag. It's far better to buy a quality trailer right from the start.

The owner fitted the interior of this trailer with toolboxes. This is a very basic, effective, and inexpensive way to maximize the use of an enclosed trailer.

continued from page 7

will you only need a trailer for short trips around town? Do you need a dressing room for showering or quarters for sleeping? Are you a timid driver, or do you have the confidence to haul a large rig across the country? Horse trailers can be much more than just a way to move a horse from point *A* to point *B*. They can be as elaborate as your house. But the more conveniences you select in a trailer, the bigger your tow vehicle needs to be. Remember that the tow vehicle and trailer go down the road as one unit, and always consider the total package.

BOAT TRAILERS

Fifty years ago, boat trailers were almost nonexistent, and most of the boat trailers that did exist had single axles with really small tires. At the time, these trailers worked just fine since most of the boats they transported were small and light.

Things have changed. It's not unusual in the present day to see a 45-foot boat being towed down the interstate at 80 miles per hour. Over the past 50 years, boats and their trailers have evolved at a tremendous rate. Trailers have gotten bigger to accommodate bigger boats. The newer trailers offer more safety and durability than could only be imagined a few decades ago.

Boat trailers consist of three main components: a frame, a hull support, and an undercarriage. The frame determines both the structural strength and appearance of the trailer. Because the frame of the boat trailer is exposed, the frame must be both strong and visually appealing.

In addition to the frame, a boat trailer needs a structure to support the hull of a boat. This hull support also allows for easy loading and unloading of the boat. There are two choices for hull support: rollers or a bunk arrangement.

Finally, the trailer undercarriage, including the axle, springs, brakes, and tires, provides weight-carrying capacity as well as shock absorption. You certainly don't want the hull of your boat pounded as you drive down the highway.

This trailer is heavy but clearly well constructed. Note the attachment points for the fender and the way the rear lights are protected. Even though the trailer was designed for hauling cars around, the option to install sides makes it useful for a lot more.

This small trailer has both a winch and a tongue jack. The winch and the two bunks are fully adjustable.

Steel versus Aluminum

Boat trailer frames are made of either steel or aluminum. Most boat trailers today are made of aluminum, which continues to grow in popularity, particularly among people who frequent salt water in hot, humid climates where rust wreaks havoc on steel. Aluminum is inherently more corrosion-resistant than steel. It also weighs less, which can help reduce the weight of the load you have to pull down the road. On the downside, an aluminum trailer will typically cost 20 to 25 percent more than a painted steel trailer and 10 to 15 percent more than a galvanized steel trailer of equal capacity.

As we gain experience with aluminum trailers, some people are switching back to steel trailer units. Some of the problems that have occurred with aluminum trailers include broken welds and even corroded frames. There have also been shearing and tearing problems in minor accidents, especially on trailers of lesser quality.

Keep in mind that one pound of steel is three times as strong as one pound of aluminum. In other words, it takes more aluminum to equal the strength of steel. Manufacturers that use aluminum have to increase the amount of aluminum used in the frame to make it as strong as a frame made of steel. Because of this, some of your better aluminum trailers will often weigh as much as a steel-built trailer. Sometimes, an aluminum trailer will even be heavier than one made of steel.

Note how the tongue is attached to the frame of trailer. Due to the trailer's construction, the tow vehicle will not just pull on the welds but will actually pull on the main frame members.

13

CARING FOR A WINCH

If you have a problem with the winch on your trailer, you might not get your boat, car, or snowmobile back onto the trailer. All boat trailers have a winch, and many others types of trailers do as well. The rules are very simple: Take care of your winch, and everything will be fine. While the suggestions here are mainly for boat owners, they do apply to other situations.

Oil the Gears

- Make sure that the winch assembly is clean.
- Apply a light coating of household oil (such as three-in-one oil) on the gears only. Don't use motor oil on the cables.
- Operate the winch when applying the oil to make sure that you get oil onto all the gear surfaces.

Inspect the Winch Strap or Cable

- Inspect your winch strap, cable, or rope every time you launch and recover your boat. Stowing your winch strap, cable, or rope evenly and neatly will extend its useful life.
- Check to make sure the bow's eye hook is secured to the strap, rope, or cable.
- At least every six months, you should completely extend the rope, cable, or nylon strap and check the entire length for cuts, burrs, rust, tears, or any other damage that could create a problem. Replace the strap, cable, or rope if it is damaged.
- Make sure that the end of the strap or cable is properly secured to the winch assembly.
- Rewind the winch.

This boat trailer uses both rollers and bunks. Everything is adjustable, which means you can set up the trailer for a variety of different hull shapes, while providing just the right amount of support for the hull of the boat. The bunk coverings are long since gone, yet the rollers are still in decent shape. You can buy a trailer in this condition cheaply and, with a minimum amount of money, have a decent trailer.

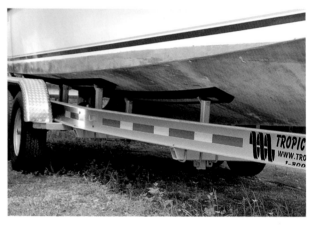

There are two ways to support a boat on a trailer: rollers or bunks. The bunk system shown here is basically some wood that's been covered in waterproof carpet. It provides more than adequate hull support for driving down the highway.

Generally, however, aluminum trailers are lighter than steel trailers. So light, in fact, they can actually float in water. Flotation occurs most often with double- and triple-axle trailers, because the air in the tires acts as a buoy for the frame. As you might imagine, a trailer that floats can create problems when it comes time to launch and retrieve a boat at the ramp. Even a mild current can shove the floating trailer sideways.

Bolted versus Welded

Some trailer companies bolt everything together. Other companies weld everything. Because aluminum trailers are generally bolted together, manufacturers often stiffen aluminum frames with a galvanized steel crossmember at the rear of the trailer.

Some people feel that bolted frames are superior to welded frames because welds immediately begin to fatigue, reducing the structural integrity of the base metal. In reality, the welds on an aluminum trailer are often the weakest point in the structure. That's the reason why stitch welding is often used in conjunction with bolted assemblies at the most critical points (over the axles and at the coupler).

While nuts and bolts might seem a bit outdated, bolting structural members together offers unmatched strength. There is always some strength loss due to the heat associated

The small aluminum flap at the end of this ramp bridges the gap between the end of the ramp and the ground, making loading and unloading easier.

with welding. Remember that heat will change the molecular structure of the aluminum. If the welding is done improperly it can actually weaken the aluminum.

Rollers versus Bunk

Rollers, which are made of either polyurethane or hard rubber, provide hull support and allow you to roll a boat onto a trailer. Bunks are generally made from wood covered with a waterproof fabric, and they allow a boat to nestle into the bed of a trailer.

If you believe that trailers shouldn't be put in the water, you've already made your decision. Rollers allow you to get the tail end of the trailer over the water without getting the trailer hubs in the water. However, if your regular boat ramp has a shallow angle, you may want to use a bunk trailer to get the boat out of the water.

Your decision on which hull support to use will ultimately depend upon the boat ramps you use. In most cases, a boat will glide on and off a roller trailer much more easily than a bunk trailer. This situation is ideal in the Midwest, where shallow ramps are common. In the South, however, reservoirs with steep ramps are more common. A bunk trailer works well on steep ramps. If you decide to purchase a bunk trailer, purchase one with pivoting bunks that tilt for easier loading.

If you go with rollers, make sure they're high-quality, nonmarking rollers that have no metal-to-metal contact that could rust and prevent the rollers from rotating. When you purchase a new trailer, you can request that extra rollers be added to the frame. The extra hull support may be worth the expense.

This ramp is way too steep for most purposes. Would you want to have to push your motorcycle up this ramp after a long day out at the track?

Power loading your boat onto a roller trailer isn't for the timid. Power loading simply means that you drive the boat onto the trailer using the boat's motor. It's a matter of aiming and manipulating the throttle. Although this technique takes practice, it works great with either bunk or roller trailers. However, power loading a deep-V hull with an inboard/outboard drive is risky on some ramps, as the prop may hit the bottom.

In those instances when you can't power load your boat, a roller trailer makes it much easier to pull the boat onto the trailer using a winch. However, you need to exercise caution with this loading technique. It is easy to get on the wrong side of the roller set and create some ugly gouges in the boat's bottom. A good set of side guides can prevent this situation.

A small rear door gives the trailer more structural rigidity, but it limits what you can put into this trailer. With this steep ramp angle, you might even need an electric winch to get the ATV into this trailer.

The toy box is the latest thing in trailers. You can load your motorcycles or ATVs in the back. When you get to your favorite recreational site, you can unload the toys, freeing up the trailer's interior for living quarters. The two horizontal platforms at the back of the trailer are bunk beds.

Here's an effective setup for hauling Jet Skis. The two spare tires indicate that the owner likes to plan for the worst-case scenario.

If you have an outboard-powered boat (especially one with power trim), then power loading on a bunk trailer is really easy. With a good set of side guides, you can do it alone without wading in the water or wrestling with the bow of the boat.

Trailer manufacturers will state that a well-designed roller trailer can support the weight of the boat just as well as a bunk trailer does. The key is to have enough rollers and to have them in the right place. Achieving this balanced setup is actually a lot harder than simply having two or four bunks.

A well-adjusted bunk trailer with side guides and sufficient tongue length is the least-expensive trailer you can buy. This trailer also requires the least amount of maintenance, and bunk systems have the least potential for damaging your boat.

When choosing a trailer, select one that allows your boat to nestle down between the fenders. This position lowers the center of gravity, resulting in a better towing rig. Keep in mind that the lower the boat is on the trailer, the quicker it will float at the boat ramp.

If you regularly use shallow ramps, you might consider putting a longer tongue on the trailer. This option adds very little cost to a new trailer yet results in a better towing rig and makes launching easier at most boat ramps. The only drawback for most folks is storage—longer trailers aren't very easy to hide in your backyard.

Remember also that longer trailers typically tow better. Actually, it would be more accurate to say that a greater separation between the rear wheels of the tow vehicle and the wheels of the trailer help stability. A longer tongue extends the axle separation for stability. The tongue of the trailer should be long enough to allow a reasonable turning radius and clearance when backing. If the tongue is short, it may be an indication of weakness or shortcuts in the design.

Axles

In general, if your boat is less than 20 feet in length, you may use a single-axle trailer. If your boat is longer than 20 feet, too much weight will be placed on the single axle, especially if driving down the highway at a high speed. If your boat is over 20 feet long, consider a dual-axle trailer. Some trailer manufacturers use a 21-foot figure; others say 23 feet or 3,000 to 3,500 pounds.

Weight Considerations

It comes as a surprise to many boat buyers that boat manufacturers generally only state dry, or empty, weights for their boats. The base weight of your boat is most likely given as the weight without options, water, or fuel. The stated weight typically doesn't include engine upgrades, which may weigh several hundred pounds more than the base powerplant. Also, the weight provided for most outboard-powered boats is only for the hull. You need to add the weight of the motor, boat trailer, and any accessories, gear, water, or fuel carried aboard.

THE ELECTRIC WINCH KIT

Electric winches are well worth the money. They cost between $200 and $400, depending on the size of your boat. Plan to spend a couple of hours installing the winch. The winch rating should be at least 75 percent of the weight of your fully loaded boat or whatever you intend to pull up on your trailer. The cable should be rated at one and a half times that figure. Remember that winches are not designed to secure the load as you drive down the road. Once you have your boat or car on the trailer, release the tension on the bow hook. Let the tie-downs do their work.

The winch kit normally contains everything you need for installation, except the tools and perhaps a couple of items you'll find at a hardware store (such as extra nuts and bolts). The easiest part of this job is mounting the winch on your trailer's winch stand.

Bolt patterns are pretty standard, and you only have to tighten a few bolts. Most electric winches use slots instead of holes for mounting. Also, most winch mounts are angled so you can adjust the height of the winch to properly clear the cable under your bow stop by sliding it up or down on the mount. In some cases, you may need to adjust the height of the winch mount to get proper clearance, and most trailers allow you to do this.

The biggest deal is that you have to get power to your winch. Wiring is usually the hardest part of this job. The good part is that wiring kits with complete instructions are available. Then there is the fact you only have two wires to deal with. How hard can this really be?

First, please read the directions that came with your wiring kit. I know it's not a manly thing to do, but it might actually help you do this job. Next, uncoil all of the wire that came in your kit. The first step is to find the wire that you're going to connect to the hot side of the battery. You can use the battery cable bolt if you have post-style terminals. If you have a side-mount battery, you can buy terminal adapters at the auto parts store that allow you to attach a wire end to the hot-side terminal.

Next, run the cable down through the engine compartment. Secure the cable with a dozen or so tie wraps. Be sure to route your harness away from things that move or get hot, and secure it with the tie wraps. Under your vehicle, you should find all kinds of handy things to secure the harness to. Brake lines are commonly run through holes in the frame, as is some wiring. You'll also need to find a bolt or a screw to serve as your ground. You'll need a drill and a self-tapping screw to complete the connection.

You'll end up with a length of wire at the rear of the vehicle that should easily reach the winch. You could coil this up and hide it inside the vehicle, but I suggest trimming the excess and wiring it to a plug. Then use a shorter cord to connect to your winch. Most manufacturers provide a short cord with two

Remember: the tow weight we need to be concerned about is the *total* weight, *not* the weight of any single item. The numbers provided by the manufacturer should only be used as a guideline. It's not unusual for a boat that the manufacturer lists at 5,000 pounds to go down the road at 6,500 or even 7,000 pounds.

Depending on the size of the boat, the trailer itself can weigh anywhere from a few hundred pounds to more than 1,500 pounds. When calculating fuel or water loads, figure about 6.1 pounds per gallon of gasoline, 7.1 pounds per gallon of diesel, and 8.3 pounds per gallon of water. It all adds up rather quickly.

The key to trouble-free towing is to match the tow vehicle with the total load. You'll need to know how much the boat and trailer truly weigh, and a scale is the best place to find out. Find a scale and weigh your rig the same way you would outfit it for a summer vacation.

MOTORCYCLE TRAILERS

There are many styles of motorcycle trailers, from covered trailers to trailers with air suspension. Some of them even fold up for easy storage when not in use. The first thing to consider when purchasing a motorcycle trailer is how many bikes will be carried on the trailer. Most people don't ride solo, which means they'll need a trailer that can handle a couple of bikes. Three-bike trailers get a little large but are available.

Many motorcycle trailers can also function as utility trailers. The ramps that hold the motorcycle tires can be unbolted to make a very nice, small utility trailer. I'm willing to bet this type of trailer sees more action at the home improvement store than it sees at motorcycle gatherings.

JET SKI TRAILERS

You may not want to own a trailer, but you really can't have a Jet Ski, or personal watercraft, without owning one. Fortunately, Jet Skis are small and their trailers can be small as well.

plugs that'll accomplish this. Keep it in the trunk, or glove box, and pull it out when you need it.

If you wire your vehicle for a winch, always spend the money to get the correct power cable from your local trailer store or the winch manufacturer. Winches use a lot of power, and it's best to use the fuse built into the cable. If you have any doubt about your wiring ability, have the trailer store wire it for you.

Instead of installing wiring for the winch, you could use battery clamps by building a custom harness and running it from the battery to the winch, simply draping it over the vehicle to use it. But by the time you've done all the work and retrieved the boat five or six times, you'll realize you would have spent less time rigging a permanent connection.

Like everything else, there are easy ways and hard ways to use your new toy to dump your boat into the water, or your ATV into the dirt. Many like to use the winch cable and the built-in clutch mechanism to control the boat's descent into the water. When you do this, you have to crawl out on the trailer, unhook the boat from the cable, fasten a line to the bow eye, and push the boat to the dock. A lot of people prefer to dump the boat with a line already attached after freeing it from the winch. You can simply walk the boat around to a parking spot with the bowline. If you have a small boat and launch in uncrowded settings, this works just fine.

The size of your boat will determine how you hook up to load it back onto your trailer. If you own a small boat, you can shove off from the dock while aboard and reach for the bow hook. With bigger boats, you might not be able to reach the bow hook. You may have to stand on your trailer and drag the boat to you with your bowline or have a friend drive the boat to you. Either way, it's best to get everyone off the boat before you winch it onto the trailer in case there's a cable failure. This applies to cars, ATVs, and snowmobiles as well. Take up any slack in the cable so it's wound firmly on the winch drum. There's no need to help the cable onto the drum. A stray broken strand of wire can leave you with a nasty cut. Keep your vehicle running while retrieving your boat, since powering the winch could drain your battery.

I haven't done much maintenance work on any of my winches, aside from occasional cable lubrication. You can use WD-40 to soak the cable as you wind it on the drum. Another alternative might be a heavy-duty marine lubricant such as Corrosion Block or Boeshield T-9. White lithium grease in the spray cans works nicely, too, but it's a little messy.

Most trailers deliver good self-centering action once the boat is firmly on the center roller. It's far easier to get your boat on the trailer straight when it's not semifloating over a sunken trailer. A power winch provides cheap insurance for your vessel, tow vehicle, and especially your trailer.

You can easily pick up these trailers by the tongue and move them around. Despite their size, Jet Ski trailers are subject to all of the basic rules and aggravations of any other trailer. They have lights that go out in the middle of the night, and if you don't grease the bearings, a wheel could fall off.

You need to hose down your Jet Ski trailer after use, especially if you play in salt water. Always rinse off the trailer when you are done for the day. This is especially critical for the lug nuts. To prevent potential problems, consider stainless-steel lug nuts, or spray the lug nuts with WD-40 once the trailer is out of the water.

Larger tires are always better, but most small trailers come with small tires. I don't advocate swapping tires, but check to see if the manufacturer offers an optional tire in a larger size.

Consider how and where you'll store your Jet Ski trailer. It's easy to just leave it parked beside the garage since it's so small, but you need to care for the tires. Raise the trailer to take the weight off of the tires. If it's going to sit unused for several months, take the tires off and put them inside your garage.

SNOWMOBILE TRAILERS

Many different types of trailers are available for transporting snowmobiles. You can shop for a number of features, but you have to consider one very important feature right from the start: How are you going to load and unload your snowmobiles?

Tilt

A tilt trailer bed tips up in the front and down in the back. This allows you to drive a snowmobile onto the trailer, but you have to drag the snowmobile off. This is the most common and least expensive trailer, but it can also be the most difficult to unload if your snowmobile doesn't have reverse or you don't have a strong back.

Note the access door at the front of this custom aluminum cover for an aluminum snowmobile trailer. For this application, aluminum works better than fiberglass, due to aluminum's lighter weight. Fiberglass snowmobile covers are generally too heavy to wrestle with, especially in the cold.

Hauling an ATV doesn't require a specialized trailer. In most cases, you can adapt a basic utility trailer to meet your needs.

Here's another clever way to maximize space: The couches/beds fold up against the wall for transport. The floor is easy to clean, and it has a nice array of tie-down locations.

The screen on this toy box trailer allows natural ventilation. The rear lights on the back are a nice touch—they allow you to work on your toys at night.

Tilt with Ramp-Off

You drive onto the back of this trailer using the tilt and then drive off the front of the trailer using ramps. This design allows you the convenience of being able to drive off the trailer without the additional expense of a drive-on/drive-off trailer. The salt shields on the front of the trailer fold down to form the ramp. These ramps are available in steel and aluminum, with aluminum being the more common choice.

Drive-On/Drive-Off

You drive onto this trailer via a ramp and drive off via a ramp. Most four-place trailers are of this design. Because most manufacturers charge a premium for convenience and additional materials, this is the most expensive type of snowmobile trailer. For a purpose-built, enclosed trailer, there are doors on both the front and back ends that form the ramps. On an open trailer, you'll have a movable common ramp or the front salt shields will double as a flip-down ramp.

Frame Materials

I recommend that you buy a trailer that is framed, sided, and covered with aluminum. Some companies offer steel trailers for slightly less money, but steel has a couple of significant limitations. First and foremost, steel trailers rust. You can slow down the rust, but it can't be totally prevented. Snowmobile trailers are subjected to the worst possible conditions: cold, water, and road salt. You can keep a steel trailer in good

A heavy-duty trailer rig like this really needs a diesel tow truck.

This travel trailer provides a small but tidy habitat for one or two people.

This is another example of a well-done package. Note how the trailer is level and the tie-downs are easy to access. The bump stops are a means of indicating how the car should be loaded for the best possible balance.

This old trailer has seen some hard use over the years. Note the handy way the ramps fold back on themselves.

shape for many years, but it will require more maintenance and expense than an aluminum trailer.

While snowmobile trailers are generally light, the overall weight of an aluminum trailer is generally less than steel. Enclosed steel trailers that can carry four sleds might weigh twice that of enclosed four-place aluminum trailers. For the money, aluminum is the best material for snowmobile trailers since it won't rust, will look better longer, and weighs less.

Enclosures

To protect your snowmobiles while on the road, you can either purchase an already-enclosed trailer or buy an enclosure as an add-on to your open trailer. The variations are endless for both types, and it pays to shop around to see what the options are.

Enclosures have many options: V-nose fronts, built-in ramps that don't need to be detached, tilt beds, and inline models. Most snowmobile owners start with an open trailer and upgrade to aftermarket covers and enclosures at a later time.

Many manufacturers produce enclosures for 10-, 12-, and 14-foot trailers. A few even make enclosures for 24- and 26-foot open trailers. The construction materials range from nylon fabric (which isn't worth buying) to high-quality aluminum and fiberglass. Aluminum enclosures are the most common and offer the greatest variety on the market. In the

Notice how the tongue of this utility trailer extends under the bed to give this trailer more than adequate strength.

last five years, smooth aluminum skin has been the hot trend and adds a very sleek appearance.

Fiberglass shells are another big trend, but they're expensive and can be very heavy. Fiberglass can also be difficult to repair if you back into a tree limb or garage opening. Nonetheless, you shouldn't discount the cool factor.

Inline Trailers

Inline trailers have become more popular. The advantage of this trailer is that it's narrower than a side-by-side trailer; you can tow it with a small vehicle and still see around it. You won't need extended mirrors with an inline trailer to maintain good visibility. On the flip side, this trailer is a long rig to tow and can be heavier than a side-by-side model. The length can also make it difficult to park in some areas. A standard two-place inline is 26 to 32 feet long, which poses storage issues as well.

Tire Selections

Larger tires are preferable for several reasons. First, larger tires dissipate heat better at highway speeds, meaning a larger tire

is less likely to blow during a long tow. A larger tire will also produce a better ride for the trailer and its contents. The small donut-style tires commonly found on snowmobile trailers are prone to blowout. Larger tires handle the highway heat better.

Most trailer companies have a standard 10-inch wheel and offer a 13-inch wheel as an option. Pay for the option. If you have a used trailer with 10-inch wheels, check around to see who makes a 13-inch wheel for your trailer.

TRAVEL TRAILERS

A travel trailer is a house you pull behind your truck. Okay, not really, but you get the idea: it's a trailer that has all of the conveniences of home. There are provisions for sleeping, showering, cooking, dining, and hanging out.

Midrange travel trailers are 18 to 25 feet long and can weigh 5,000 pounds or more. They're generally towed with a compact V-8-powered pickup truck or SUV. They have most of the amenities of the larger travel trailers but sleep fewer people than the large units.

The pop-up-style travel trailer works well for camping trips. The roof expands upward to provide a habitat. For transport, the roof folds down, making it smaller and more aerodynamic.

Travel trailers that are lightweight enough to be towed by a small SUV have recently been introduced. These lightweight versions of towable travel trailers retain all the modern conveniences of the traditional trailers. Some even offer special features like the slideout, where part of the wall extends out when you reach the RV park. Typically, lightweight towables are under 26 feet long, weigh less than 4,000 pounds, and retail from about $8,000 to $14,000.

Another recent innovation is a travel trailer called the "toy box" or "toy hauler" that's half living area and half garage. These trailers allow you to bring your toys right along with you. A folding rear ramp gives you access to your motorcycles, ATVs, personal watercraft, and even race cars. A built-in generator provides power for A/C, TV, and microwave.

CHAPTER 2
WHY DO YOU REALLY WANT A TRAILER?

You probably think you need a trailer for one specific purpose. But once you have a trailer, you'll probably want to use it for a variety of purposes. It's best to consider this right from the beginning.

Take a minute to think about all of your needs and possible uses for a trailer. You know your friends will want to borrow it on occasion. Even your spouse and his or her friends will think of reasons to use the trailer. If your situation is like most, the trailer will inevitably be used for a lot of things, such as moving furniture and hauling leaves, rocks, and other equipment.

Ask yourself the following questions before you start writing a check.

- How big a trailer do I need?
  o Width: How wide should the trailer be? Also, what are the legal limitations in my area?
  o Length (this is really a storage issue more than a towing issue): Where will I store the trailer?
- What load capacity is required? One thousand pounds? Three thousand pounds? Six thousand pounds? Even more?
- Is the bed height a factor? How will I get things on and off the trailer?
- Does the trailer need sides, or will sides just get in the way?
- Does it need a top?
- Will I need loading ramps?

MAKE A LIST

Buying a trailer is really about making a list. Write down why you need a trailer and what you might use it for. Then share the list with the rest of your family members, and see what they can add to it. You can't buy a trailer that meets all of your family's needs, but you can at least engage the family in this enterprise.

Both of these trailers haul race cars to the track; other than that, they have very little in common. Two people with the same primary goal in mind can arrive at two totally different solutions.

Notice how the tongue members go back under the bed of this well-constructed trailer. The placement of the tongue jack isn't ideal, though. When the weight of the trailer is on the tongue jack, the weight will also be a little off center.

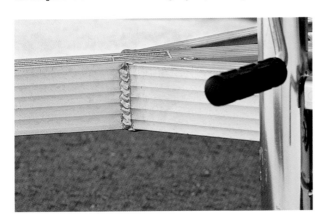

Weld quality is one sign of a company that cares, and these are good, strong welds.

This coupler is bolted to an aluminum trailer frame. Some people prefer welded to bolted, but there is very little difference in actual use.

What Will You Carry?

Write down everything you think you might need to carry with the trailer. Will your riding mower actually fit in the trailer you intend to buy?

How Big Should It Be?

Is the bed height, width, or length a factor? When it comes to utility trailers, you really need to look at a basic width of 5 to 6 feet. Anything less than 5 feet wide is just silly. Now, once you're at 5 feet, why not just go to 6? Where do you stop?

Does It Need Sides?

Consider what other options the trailer might need. A top? A tailgate? Ramps? Tie-down attachments? If you intend to tow your riding mower, you'll need ramps.

How Long Should It Last?

Do you really need a top-of-the-line utility trailer? Should it be built tough for long service, or can it be just a cheap trailer that you'll only use for light loads a few times a year?

There are a lot of things to like here: The coupler is welded to the trailer tongue, and the tongue jack has a nice wide foot to prevent it from sinking into the pavement or ground.

Known as a beaver tail, this trailer style makes loading a car just a little easier. Note that the rear lights are somewhat exposed and have no solid protection. It'd be pretty easy to knock one of these lights off.

Extra features like this front bin can make your trailer even more useful.

A little polyurethane varnish will protect this decking against scratches.

Several examples of the quality you should be looking for can be found on this trailer. First, the tie-down fixture is fully welded into the bed of the trailer. Second, the hinge on the ramp door is full-length and sturdy. Third, the recessed light is mounted in a rubber grommet.

How Will You Store It?

Most people store their trailers a lot more than they actually use them. If you only need a light, single-axle trailer, your life will be a lot easier with a collapsible trailer, even if it means you have to make two trips to the home improvement store instead of one.

HOW WILL YOU TOW THIS TRAILER?

It's really important to consider how you're going to tow a new trailer. Will you be towing it with the family car? Maybe your front-wheel-drive minivan? Or do you have a huge SUV?

In the past, I've rented a truck to tow my trailer. It was simply cheaper to rent a truck a half-dozen times a year than to have another vehicle in the driveway. I can hide the trailer in the side yard, but it's a little more difficult to hide a truck. (Actually, I suppose I could hide the truck, but my wife would find it. Then I would have to explain to her why I spent $50,000 on a truck I only need five or six times a year.)

This is what will happen if you let your trailer spend too much time in salt water. To avoid this, rinse everything down with fresh water as soon as you leave the boat ramp.

29

I prefer crossing the tie-downs, rather than running them straight back. The welded tie-down points must make life easier for this owner.

Tilt-bed trailers save you the trouble of dealing with ramps. Just make sure to keep all the pivot points lubricated.

Buyer beware: This brand-new trailer started rusting even before someone purchased it.

This is an example of quality craftsmanship; every single item is nicely executed. This is a motorcycle trailer, but with the removal of eight bolts it becomes a wonderful utility trailer. All you need to do is unscrew the wing nuts to remove the tire racks.

The trailer has to meet your basic needs, but it also has to be the right size for the vehicle that will pull it. Minivans aren't very good at pulling triple-axle trailers. Heck, minivans aren't very good at pulling anything. Are you looking at buying more than just a trailer? Buying a trailer is one thing. Buying a trailer and a giant Ford F-350 Dually puts your purchase, and your family dynamics, on a whole different level.

Questions about the tow vehicle actually become a good guide for trailer size. Every vehicle has a towing capacity. Check your owner's manual to see if your needs can be met with the car or truck you have in your driveway. If you're buying a new vehicle, ask a lot of questions, because the average dealer will try to sell you what he or she has in inventory, not necessarily what you need. The dealership may not be the best place to

find honest advice about trailer towing. On the other hand, a trailer store that doesn't sell cars and trucks can help a lot. The workers there have heard a lot about tow vehicles from their customers, and they're more than happy to share these stories. For more information on tow vehicles, see Chapter 3.

Here are some additional questions to think about with respect to towing:

- What vehicle(s) will tow the trailer?
- What's the towing capacity of the vehicle(s) I currently have?
- Can a trailer hitch be mounted to any of these vehicles?
- What's the height of the hitch point?
- Will my trailer need brakes? Will these brakes be hydraulic or electric?

WHERE WILL YOU STORE THIS TRAILER?

Storage is a very big deal. Most of the time, this trailer is going to be resting someplace. Very few of us use our trailers every day. You'd better give storage some thought before you drag a new trailer home.

- Is the access to where I will store the trailer convenient and easy, or will it make the trailer difficult to use?
- Will this trailer be stored in a garage?
- If I keep it in a garage, will I need to tip the trailer on its side or end to make room for a car? Or, will I attempt to put my wife's car in the driveway?
- Will I have to store the trailer outside?
- If I leave it outside, how will I protect it from the wind, rain, snow, and sun?
- How much space do I really have for trailer storage?

It makes very little difference whether you build a trailer or purchase something new; this investment (at least that's what you told your wife it was) is well worth protecting. On the other hand, if you can scrounge a cheap trailer that meets your needs, shelter may not be an issue. Keep in mind that the appearance of your trailer says a lot about the quality of your operation. A rusted, nasty trailer may not be the image you want to project.

SHOULD YOU BUY A TRAILER, OR SHOULD YOU BUILD ONE?

This question is a classic, and the answer is also a classic: It depends. At this point, you should have a pretty good idea of what you need. Now, find out if you can accomplish that with a purchased trailer. If not, consider building one.

Realistically, there aren't many good reasons to build your own trailer. First, you'll spend a lot of time building one. Second, it's probably going to cost you as much to make a trailer as it would to buy one. It's usually not cheaper to build your own trailer. Factories have economies of scale for purchasing raw materials and components, and they have jigs to build the trailers quickly and efficiently.

If you can wait a little bit, most trailer companies allow you to customize your trailer. Instead of just buying one off *continued on page 35*

This basic box trailer has been constructed inexpensively but not cheaply, and the tongue jack is located properly.

Again, the clue to quality lies in the details. Notice how the corners on all of the trim pieces match perfectly.

The plastic rollers wear out after a few years in the sun, but they're easily replaced. This is a good place for mounting the spare tire—it won't be in your way and you won't bang your knees on it as you work around the trailer.

The giant U-bolts can be loosened to allow the winch to be raised and lowered along the winch tower.

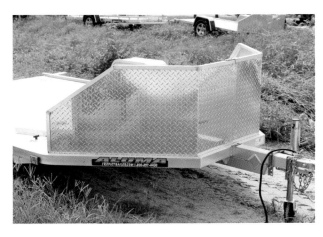

This very small, light trailer is very strong. Notice how the tongue is fabricated. All of the gussets are completely welded along the edge, instead of just spot-welded.

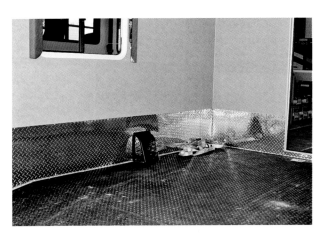

Running the diamond plate up along the wall in this toy box is a great idea. It's a lot easier to mop the floor if you don't have to worry about the trailer's lower wall.

If you only need a trailer a couple of times a year, you can save a lot of money by just renting one. Rental trailers tend to be sturdy—and heavy. They have to be to survive being hauled around by inexperienced amateurs.

continued from page 31
the lot, ask the dealer if you can add custom features. The manufacturer may be able to build you the perfect trailer. (Okay, an almost perfect trailer.) There's also a good chance the manufacturer will be able to do this for not much more than you would pay for the steel and welding to do it yourself.

Before you start thinking of your trailer as a project, stop and add up the number of unfinished projects you already have around the house. Do you really need one more project?

There are a few good reasons to embark on a trailer construction venture:
• You want something so special that it simply can't be purchased. You have some very unique needs for a trailer.
• You want to add options that simply aren't available on the market.
• You want a cool project that you can be proud of and one that people will admire.
• You want the prestige and feeling of self-worth that goes with saying you built this thing yourself.

This poor trailer has been beaten and abused. Yet it still functions. The steel tongue jack handle and the aluminum jack body have obviously been subjected to the same abuse and lack of care, yet the jack body still looks decent.

Trailers don't have to be pretty to work properly, but this is what happens after half a dozen owners over several decades. Although this tire may suffer from overinflation, the wear across the tread face is almost perfect.

Now, if you have the skills, go ahead and build it, and create that perfect trailer that you've always wanted. It can be a fun project, and you'll have something to be proud of. Just realize that you're probably not saving any money. For more information on building a trailer, see Chapter 12.

RENTING VERSUS BUYING

Many people forget that it could actually be much smarter to rent a trailer than to own one. A lot of people want a sense of ownership when it comes to a trailer; others have an obsession with personalizing their trailers. Still others simply don't want the hassle of planning ahead and having to go pick up a trailer when they decide they want to use it.

It all really comes down to how often you actually intend to use this trailer. The more you use your trailer, the greater the advantages are for owning it. If you only use it once or twice a year for a short time, then renting

makes financial sense. Consider the pros and cons in the accompanying table.

The Issue	Renting	Purchase
Ownership	no	yes
Monthly payments	no	yes
Tax deduction	no	maybe
Cost of long-term use	high	lower
Limited selection	yes	no
Require a reservation	yes	no
Maintenance	no	yes
Customizable	no	yes
Availability	very limited	very good

THE USED TRAILER

I'm cheap. I've bought over a dozen used trailers in my lifetime. I've even bought a couple that I never hooked up

Fenders tend to take the biggest beating. Fenders that are bolted into place are easier to replace.

Everything you see on this beat-up trailer can be replaced easily. If the axle and frame of a boat trailer are solid, then it's not very difficult to rebuild the trailer to like-new condition.

to a tow vehicle. Tires, load capacity, and lights are the most important points to review on a used trailer.

Tires

The most important items to look at when considering the purchase of a used trailer are the wheels and tires. Okay, just the tires. Wheels are usually indestructible, so if the wheels look seriously abused, you can bet the whole trailer has been through the wringer. At the same time, remember that ugly is not the same as bad. Wheels can look terrible and still be perfectly functional.

Also keep in mind that a new set of tires may equal the price you paid for the entire trailer. First, check to see if the tires on the trailer are actually trailer tires and not just cheap car tires. Trailer tires can make all the difference when it comes to towing.

Next, determine how old the tires are. Very few people ever wear out trailer tires. Instead, the tires fail because of old age. Unfortunately, they usually fail on the expressway at 70 miles per hour. See Chapter 6 for information on how to read the date codes on a trailer's tires. If the tires on the trailer you covet are more than five years old, you should plan on replacing them.

Load Capacity

Next, figure out how much this bargain trailer can carry. I love the articles that tell you to check the placard on the trailer. Most of the time, you'll be lucky if the trailer is even registered. If you can't determine the load capacity of the trailer, then you can make an estimate by looking at the number of axles under the trailer bed and counting the number of lug nuts on the wheels. Don't forget that tires are also a huge factor in determining the load capacity of your trailer. Chapter 6 will help you decipher all of this information.

Lights

Next, check the trailer lights. The easiest way is to ask the seller to back his tow vehicle up to the trailer and connect the plug. If he can't do that, then it probably means he's trying to sell you a lousy trailer. For more information on trailer lights, see Chapter 10.

Check Out the Maximum Towing Capacity of Your Tow Vehicle

This information is on the driver's doorpost or in the owner's manual. Your vehicle will determine what sort of trailer you purchase. It's all too easy to buy a trailer that requires a brand-new tow vehicle. Don't make an accidental purchase of that sort. The family usually isn't too excited when you announce that you need a new truck to tow the trailer you just bought—and that you'll have to dine on macaroni and cheese and canned soup until the new truck has been paid off.

Determine the Maximum Load That You'll Be Hauling

If you are hauling horses, the load is based on the weight of the horses you'll carry. If you plan on hauling race cars around, add the weight of the car and all of the extra junk you'll pile on before leaving for the drag strip.

Also identify the unloaded weight of any trailer you're considering. This should be stamped on the trailer. But if it's not, you might have to make a guess. Remember: The unloaded weight of the trailer plus the maximum load capacity of the trailer is the total weight that you'll tow. If that total is more than your vehicle's maximum towing capacity, you need to either adjust your plans or get a larger tow vehicle.

Make Sure That You Understand Trailer Design

The smallest trailers have a single axle (although large single-axle trailers exist). Many of these are capable of hauling only small loads, such as modest-sized recreational boats, snowmobiles, and personal watercraft. Single-axle trailers are very easy to move around when they're unhitched. Double-axle trailers usually have a higher load capacity and always ride more smoothly than single-axle trailers. The additional wheels add stability when the trailer is unhitched. Double-axle trailers are used for large sailboats and car haulers but aren't very easy to move around in your driveway. Triple-axle trailers haul very large loads, such as tractors, and are impossible to maneuver by hand due to their long wheelbase.

Decide Which Type of Trailer Connection You Really Want

Trailers that connect to the back of a vehicle are generally called tag-along trailers. Most tag-along trailers require a hitch that mounts to the vehicle frame. The really big trailers use a fifth-wheel, or gooseneck, mount that can be used only with a pickup truck that has a permanent hitch mount installed. These trailers ride more smoothly than tag-alongs, but they're not cheap to buy or maintain. They won't help your fuel mileage, either.

Decide on Your Target Budget and Stick to It

There are some really good used trailer bargains out there. The only thing that depreciates faster than a trailer is a motorhome. Smaller trailers seem to run about $1,000, although I still hunt down the $500 ones. A medium-capacity, double-axle trailer costs about $3,000. Fully enclosed trailers are more expensive. There's really almost no limit on the top-end trailers. I've seen a 48-foot trailer that cost well over $45,000—and that was a used trailer.

USED TRAVEL TRAILERS

Used travel trailers are a special case, since they have a myriad of systems. You have all of the basic trailer components, plus all of the systems usually found in your home. The potential problems can be daunting. Remember, you usually don't get a warranty with a used trailer. Once you hook it up and drive away, you're on your own. Look at a lot of trailers. Check out the used lots at all the trailer dealers in your area. Check online listings, too; the two most commonly used are Craigslist and eBay. These online sales are now the most common way to search for a used travel trailer, but keep in mind that shopping online is probably going to involve some travel to inspect the trailer you're thinking about buying.

I like to think that buying a used travel trailer is a lot like buying a used truck. It's not about finding the perfect truck; it's about walking away from a lot of trucks that could be a problem. Anyone can write a check. It takes a lot more fortitude to walk away from a truck, or travel trailer, that's almost what you're looking for.

After a half-dozen trailer inspections, you'll develop a procedure for checking out a trailer. If you're really smart and organized, you'll even make up your own checklist. Make some notes, and keep a file of the trailers you've walked away from. There's a very good chance that this trailer will still be for sale six months from your initial inspection. Sometimes, the trailer you initially turned down might be, upon reflection, the one you decide to purchase.

Start your inspection with a basic walk around. You already know about tires and wheels from earlier in this book. Now's the time to put that knowledge to use. As you walk around the trailer, look for screws that are loose and banged-up trim pieces. Do you see a lot of dents and rust? Get down on

continued on page 42

RV TRAILER INSPECTION CHECKLIST

Trailer Brand: _____

Date of Manufacture: _____

Serial Number: _____

Trailer Length: _____

Location of Trailer: _____

Owner's Name: _____

Owner's Phone Number: _____

Owner's email address: _____

Exterior

Roof Sealing: Check the sealing on seams, gaskets, and screw heads. Check around the air conditioning vents, antennas, sewer vents, and side seams.

Notes: _____

_____

Doors: Check all the door gaskets for a positive seal. Check the alignment of the door.

Notes: _____

_____

Exterior Compartments: Check the operation of doors and the mechanism for holding the doors open. Make sure the hinges are tight and secure. Check that doors close tightly. Check for moisture stains and leaks. Check the operation of the compartment lights.

Notes: _____

_____

Generator Compartment: Check the door for alignment and tight fit. Check that everything is tight and rattle-free. Make sure that the exhaust is not under a window or a slide. Operate the power slide a few times to make sure it works.

Notes: _____

_____

_____

Utility Compartment: Check closely how each valve works. Look at how the sewer hose is stored. Check the proper function of black and gray valves. Understand how tank flushing works. Check the water filters for proper installation. Check the electrical reel operation. Check the telephone and cable connections for a satellite dish.

Notes: _____

_____

_____

Propane: Check for downward ventilation. Make sure that the tank is secure. Check that propane cannot enter the trailer. Check the operation of the main shutoff.

Notes: _____

_____

_____

Tires and Wheels: Inspect all the tires for proper inflation. Also look for uneven tread wear on the tires.

Notes: _____

_____

_____

Windows: Check the exterior of each window for alignment and proper seals.

Notes: _____

_____

Paint: Check carefully for bubbles, pits, and chips. Examine any vinyl film for bubbles. Look for paint overspray, which might indicate prior damage. Check the surface for smoothness.

Notes: _____

_____

Awnings: Operate the awnings several times. Check the springs, locks, and supports for alignment. Check the fabric for tears and punctures. If the awnings are equipped with wind sensors, check them with compressed air while the awnings are extended.

Notes: _____

_____

_____

Chassis Inspection: Check both the wiring and plumbing for proper fastening. Check to make sure that undercoating hasn't been sprayed on the brake calipers. Check the brake calipers for stains, which would indicate a brake fluid leak. Look for fluid leaks.

Notes: _____

_____

_____

_____

Slide-Out Operation: Check the seals while the slide is retracted. Operate each slide several times. Understand the interlocks that might be present. Check the manual retraction process. Check for the proper alignment of wheels and for clearance. Check any locking mechanisms for proper operation and alignment. Make sure the seals are properly installed and operational when the slide is retracted and extended.

Notes: _____

_____

_____

_____

Interior Fit and Finish

Cabinets: Examine the outside of all the cabinets for scratches, nicks, and loose handles. Check that all hinges and latches operate properly. Pull drawers all the way out several times. Try to open them like road vibration would.

Notes: _____

_____

Lighting: Operate every light switch. Operate battery disconnect switches.

Notes: _____

_____

_____

Closets: Check the operation of all the doors and their alignment. Make sure that all the hanger rods are securely fastened. Check all of the closet lighting and any switches that are provided.

Notes: _____

_____

Furniture: Check the furniture for construction, upholstery, pattern, and cloth matching. Check out the dinette by making it into a bed.

Notes: _____

_____

Blinds: Operate all the window blinds and check their alignment. Check that all the window valances and trim are secure.

Notes: _____

_____

Countertops: Check all the countertops for alignment and correct fastening. Check that all the trim pieces are there and tight. Check the caulking for quality anywhere water egress is possible. Look at the quality of the sink and faucet installation.

Notes: _____

_____

Windows: Operate every window and window lock. Inspect and operate each emergency window. Locks and latches should work freely but securely.

Notes: _____

_____

Floor Coverings: Check all carpeting and floor coverings to see that they are properly fastened down. Check to make sure the grout in the tile flooring is complete and clean. Check under any sliding cabinets.

Notes: _____

_____

Wall Coverings: Check all wall coverings to ensure that the joints meet properly. Check for nicks, scratches, and tears.

Notes: _____

_____

Operational Test of Systems

Generator: Have the owner show you how to start and stop the generator. Know where the remote stations are located and how they work. Start the generator, and listen for unusual noises or vibrations. Understand any power relays, and test incoming AC power prior to cutting through. Check the electrical status panel. Put a load on the generator by running the microwave, turning on and off all AC-powered lights. Let the generator run for 10 or 15 minutes.

Notes: _____

_____

_____

Inverter/Converter/Charger: Understand the operation. Have the owner explain the function of all controls, displays, and lights. Check that batteries are being charged. Shut down the generator. Leave the inverter in the on position. Check to see that the inverter took over all AC voltages. Test by turning on the microwave for a minute. Turn on the TV, and leave it on for the rest of the inspection.

Notes: _____

_____

Water Pump: Make sure that the freshwater tank has water. Turn on the pump, and listen for the pump to start. After the pump stops, open the faucet and let it run until the pump starts, and then close the faucet. Listen for noisy, vibrating pipes or pipes that make irritating sounds.

Notes: _____

_____

Water Heater: Test the operation of the water heater while on propane. Then test the operation using electricity. Turn off the water heater when done.

Notes: _____

_____

Furnace: Have the owner demonstrate the operation of the thermostat as it relates to heating and cooling. Check the operation of the furnace. You should have heat coming from all vents after a few minutes. Check for the smell of any material getting hot.

Notes: _____

_____

LP, Carbon Monoxide, Smoke Alarms: Have the owner test each one of these items and explain the testing procedure.

Notes: _____

_____

Refrigerator: Understand the controls and status lights. Set the unit to propane, and check outside to see that the heating column is lit and heating. Set the temperature to its highest setting, and come back to see if the coils are cooling after about 10 minutes.

Notes: _____

_____

_____

TV/VCR Antenna and Switching: Test the raising, lowering, and rotating of the TV antenna system. If there is a DSS satellite system, test it out. Make sure you understand the operation of all the remotes.

Notes: _____

_____

_____

Air Conditioners: After the generator has stabilized, turn on the front air-conditioning unit. After a few minutes, cool air should be coming out the vents. Switch the unit over to heat mode and check for heat after a few minutes. Walk around, and make sure that air comes from all vents. Leave this system running for a while.

Notes: _____

_____

Air Vents: Check the operation of both kitchen and bath vents. Check that both vents close and retract tightly.

Notes: _____

_____

Microwave: With the air conditioner running, heat a cup of water for 3 minutes. The generator should hold strong, and the water should be hot.

Notes: _____

_____

Propane Stove: Check the operation of one burner while the microwave is running. Turn on other burners and note if there's adequate propane flow to the burners. Operate the oven.

Notes: _____

_____

continued from page 38

the ground and look for dents and rust under the trailer. Use a flashlight to check the frame. You should be looking for anything unusual under the trailer. Look for dangling wires and wires that have been spliced together. Check to see if any parts of the frame appear to have been replaced or bent. Most people will clean their trailer for sale but very few bother to deal with issues found under the trailer. That means the bottom of the trailer may be the single best indication of how well the trailer's been maintained.

Now look in all of the exterior compartments. Do you see water stains? Are they filthy? These exterior compartments are really good indicators of the condition of the total trailer. If a person has kept these in good condition, then he or she probably took good care of the rest of the trailer.

If there are pullouts and awnings, ask the owner to operate them. Are the awnings stained? Do you see mildew on them? How easy are they to operate? If the awnings are operated electrically, give them a little workout. Put them up and down several times to see to how well they handle it. On the slideouts, check the condition of the seals when the slide is retracted. Next, pretend that the automatic retraction mechanism is broken, and ask the owner to demonstrate the manual retraction process. In the process, you'll learn a lot about how the slides on this trailer operate.

As you move into the trailer, check the condition of the steps and the door. Are the hinges in good shape? How about the screening on the door? Open and close the door a few times from the inside. Does the door work to your satisfaction? Remember: You're looking for reasons not to buy this trailer. Be harsh. Be very critical of every flaw you find. You don't have to announce each and every flaw to the owner, just make a note on your checklist.

Now, walk around inside the trailer. Open and close every single window. Do they work? If so, how well? Do they all have screens? Can you lock them? Replacing windows gets very expensive very quickly. Pay particular attention to the safety egress windows, since these have probably never been used.

Now, go around and check the plumbing. Do all of the faucets work? Are there any leaks? Go into the bathroom and close the door. Will your family have enough room?

Removable fenders are great to have on a trailer. The wing nuts make removing the fenders a snap. No wrenches needed.

Check out the condition of the furniture. Is it stained and worn out? Is the bed comfortable? If you don't like it now, you certainly won't like it six months from now. Nothing in this used trailer is going to get better unless you fix it yourself out of your own pocket. All of the little problems you're seeing now will be larger and more annoying in the future.

Now, ask the owner to start the generator and explain the control panel. It's worth checking the operation of each electrical outlet. If you don't have one already, you can get a handy outlet tester at any hardware or home improvement store. Turn on all the lights, and then operate the microwave for several minutes. You want to actually strain the electrical system. It's better to find a problem before you write that check.

If all of this seems a little brutal, it probably is. Remember, it's not about the trailer that you buy. It's really all about how many problematic trailers you can walk away from. It's up to the current owner to make excuses for any problems that you might run across. Your job is to find the problems. Actually, you can either find these problems now, or you can find them in the middle of Montana.

CHAPTER 3
WHAT WILL YOU USE TO TOW YOUR TRAILER?

There's no such thing as a perfect tow vehicle. I've had good ones, and I've had really bad ones. Yet even those bad ones did what was required of them. If you're buying new, find a truck or SUV that can tow more than what you think you'll be towing. It'll take less effort to tow a 5,000-pound trailer with a vehicle rated to tow 8,500 pounds than it will to tow that 5,000 pounds with a vehicle rated to tow just 5,000 pounds. You'll be glad to have that extra towing capacity if you decide to carry any additional equipment or step up to a larger trailer or heavier load. You can overdo it, though: Buying a Ford F-350 diesel to tow a 12-foot aluminum boat is just plain silly.

Whatever the case, rule #1 in this process is to never exceed the gross vehicle weight rating (GVWR) of the tow vehicle. This rating is the maximum allowable total weight of the tow vehicle itself plus the cargo, fuel, and passengers. This weight includes the curb weight of the vehicle, payload, and hitch weight. Hitch weight is the percentage of the trailer weight that is placed on the trailer coupler of the tow vehicle.

Most U.S. cars have a placard (sticker) with the GVWR information. It's generally located either in the driver-side door or doorframe. It may also be present on another sticker immediately under the hood near the radiator, although that sticker typically contains information about the size of the motor, various fluid capacities, and so on. When all else fails, look in the owner's manual.

Gross weight is often confused with curb weight, which represents the weight of the vehicle without passengers or cargo.

continued on page 48

As with any used vehicles, older trucks can be a real bargain—or an absolute nightmare.

Heavy-duty trucks are great for pulling just about anything you might own, but these big trucks can be a bear to park.

The Ford F-250 is a true workhorse. The diesel-equipped model can tow just about anything. At the same time, it's suitable for everyday use.

Crew cabs allow you to take the whole family in comfort.

This dedicated tow truck is designed to do one thing and one thing only: tow huge trailers.

Notice how level the trailer is at 70 miles per hour.

You don't need a big truck for your basic utility trailer, although this combination needs a better weight balance. The trailer's front end and the truck's back end are both raised rather than level. The combination is almost V-shaped as it goes down the road.

The utility trailer is dead parallel to the road at 70 miles per hour. Proper weight balance is the key to achieving this.

This light trailer and light SUV are roughly the same size, and form a well-matched combination.

Notice how far to the rear of the trailer the wheels are located. In this situation, optional extended mirrors become important.

Although empty trailers bounce around and make a lot of noise, an empty boat trailer won't hurt your gas mileage or block your vision to the rear.

continued from page 43

Just to clarify: The difference between gross weight and curb weight is the total passenger and cargo weight capacity of the vehicle. For example, a pickup truck with a curb weight of 6,000 pounds might have a cargo capacity of 3,000 pounds, meaning it can have a gross weight of 9,000 pounds when fully loaded.

Tow vehicles also have a gross axle weight rating (GAWR) limit. Payload and hitch weight must be divided evenly between the axles to conform to the maximum weight limits and to prevent problems driving down the road, swaying from lane to lane.

WHEELBASE

The longer the wheelbase on your tow vehicle, the easier it will be to tow a trailer. Longer is better, plain and simple. Think of it as leverage. The longer the trailer, the more

leverage this trailer can have on the tow vehicle. The longer the wheelbase of the tow vehicle, the more the tow vehicle can resist the leverage being applied by the trailer. I'm probably stating the obvious here, but remember that it's better to have the tow vehicle controlling the trailer than it is to have the trailer controlling the tow vehicle.

This doesn't mean you need a crew cab, long-bed truck to pull a pop-up camping trailer. A small SUV can easily tow a small trailer. But that same small SUV won't be able to handle towing a 30-foot trailer. That size trailer will require a longer tow vehicle.

It is a fact that short-wheelbase tow vehicles are easier to maneuver than longer ones. However, a longer-wheelbase vehicle has much greater high-speed stability and ride comfort. In a nutshell, a long trailer on a short-wheelbase tow vehicle is not a good thing.

From a safety standpoint, a longer wheelbase gives you more resistance to jackknifing, the tendency for the tow vehicle to brake faster in a panic stop than the trailer. In a jackknifing situation, the tow vehicle starts to slow down while the trailer keeps right on coming and tries to make the "jackknife" blade swing shut by forcing the tow vehicle to swap ends. The results are usually very ugly.

In terms of safe towing, wheelbase is a crucial consideration. If you tow with a short-wheelbase vehicle and have no trailer brakes (or they don't work properly), you could be in for trouble.

The first 110 inches of your tow vehicle's wheelbase allow you roughly 20 feet of trailer. For each additional 4 inches of tow truck wheelbase, you can add another foot of trailer. See the chart for more information. Keep in mind that this chart is a guideline for trailer length, not a hard-and-fast set of rules.

Rust is the main problem with steel trailers.

Aluminum boat trailers are lightweight and won't rust.

The total weight of the trailer is also a huge factor when it comes to safe, stable towing. Even the type of tires you use on your tow vehicle (light truck versus passenger car) can play a huge role in stability. For tow vehicles, the distance from the coupler to the rear trailer axle should be no more than twice the wheelbase of the tow vehicle. See the chart on page 50 for more information.

ENGINE

Keep in mind that as soon as you hook a 25-foot sailboat behind your vehicle, you're nearly doubling the demands on every part of the vehicle—certainly the engine. Assuming your tow vehicle plus the loaded trailer weighs 3,500 to 7,000 pounds, you should understand that you're asking the engine to move about twice the weight as soon as you drop the hitch onto the ball. That's a whole lot more weight. Any engine that's underpowered for the task is going to be stressed. A stressed engine isn't going to have any reserve power for passing. Don't even think about going up steep hills.

What if you already have lots of power? You can expect that the tow vehicle will still run hotter than normal and use a lot more gas. Really big engines never get very good gas mileage to begin with. Hitch a trailer on the back and your mileage is going to be even worse.

Medium-sized engines may get only 60 percent of the fuel economy they do when not towing. In fact, smaller engines might even be worse on gas than larger engines when towing. Why the significant difference? Medium-sized engines are working really hard. You have to put your foot into it to maintain speed, particularly up grades. Every time you push down on the pedal, you can almost watch the gas gauge needle move toward empty.

Is a V-6 or straight-six enough power? It depends. There are plenty of people who routinely tow with Cherokees, Astros, Aerostars, and Explorers with 4-liter V-6s and say that they feel comfortable. Then again, they're only pulling a 2,000-pound trailer. I have an open-wheel race car that I tow on a single-axle open trailer. I think I could probably tow it with a Toyota Corolla. As with everything, common sense and individual judgment play an important role.

The biggest factor in engine choice is how the vehicle is used. If towing the boat is only a very small part of its yearly duties, a V-6 may be an adequate choice. If you take a lot of long-distance trailer trips that account for the majority of the vehicle's use, a V-8 is definitely suggested.

WHAT ABOUT DIESELS?

There's a reason nearly all commercial tractor trailers are powered by diesel engines. Diesels have at least two advantages: first, fuel economy; and second, sheer pulling power. By design, diesels squeeze about 12 to 15 percent more power out of a given amount of fuel. A diesel engine with the same approximate horsepower rating as a gasoline engine will get 12 to 15 percent better mileage.

Another big advantage of the diesel engine is its performance. A diesel typically develops its maximum horsepower and torque at a much lower engine rpm than a gas engine. Not only does this contribute to longevity of internal components; it also makes a significant difference in the vehicle's towing capabilities. The diesel's torque band is wide and starts at a lower rpm range. Remember that old saying, "You advertise horsepower, but you drive torque"? Once you've towed a trailer with a diesel engine, you'll probably never go back to a gas engine.

Of course, the initial purchase price of a diesel engine can be a shocker. Selecting a diesel engine for the Ford F-250 can add almost $5,000 to the price. You have to do the math over the life of the vehicle to see if the increased power and fuel economy represent a payback.

The other downside of diesel engines can be maintenance and repair. Modern diesels and fuel-injected gas engines are similar in that they don't require much periodic maintenance beyond oil changes, filters, and so on. But, if you need repairs done on a diesel engine, it will likely cost more than a gasoline engine. Some components (such as a worn-out injector pump) are horribly expensive.

That said, chances are a diesel engine will outlast a gasoline engine by a long shot, especially when there's a lot of towing involved. Many people who tow big boats or fifth-wheel trailers routinely work their diesels up to 250,000 or even 300,000 miles without major repairs. You just can't get this kind of durability from a gasoline engine if you subject it to the severe service of towing.

TRANSMISSION

Most owners' manuals have detailed tables for determining towing requirements. If you look at your manual, you'll see

This traditional receiver is very structurally sound.

Huge tow trucks must go to a truck facility for maintenance. Wheels and tires this large are simply beyond the abilities of the average neighborhood repair shop.

that there are usually lower gross vehicle weights (GVW) and gross combination weights (GCW) for manual-transmission vehicles. From a dead stop to about 25 miles per hour, the torque converter in an automatic-transmission vehicle allows something the engineers call "torque multiplication." Simply put, torque multiplication effectively gives you lower (higher numerically) total gearing. It's almost like a lower low gear. This setup gives an automatic-transmission vehicle a noticeable advantage in starting from a dead stop, a situation you might find yourself in when pulling a loaded trailer out of the water.

With a manual transmission, you don't have torque multiplication and you'll too often have to feather the clutch a bit as you pull out of a ramp or start up uphill from a stoplight. This technique will definitely shorten the life of the clutch.

REAR AXLE RATIO

Lots of people with pickups, vans, Suburbans, Explorers, Cherokees, and similar vehicles base their perceived towing abilities on the marketing slogan "capable of towing X,XXX pounds when properly equipped." Unfortunately, most people don't bother to find out exactly what "properly equipped" means.

TOW VEHICLE WHEELBASE TO TRAILER LENGTH GUIDELINES

Wheelbase (inches)	Trailer Length (feet)	Wheelbase (inches)	Trailer Length (feet)
110	20	150	30
114	21	154	31
118	22	158	32
122	23	162	33
126	24	166	34
130	25	170	35
134	26	174	36
138	27	178	37
142	28	182	38
146	29	186	39

(This guideline was first used by the RV Consumers Group.)

REAR AXLE TO COUPLER LENGTH SUGGESTIONS

Wheelbase (inches)	Length (feet, inches)	Wheelbase (inches)	Length (feet, inches)
110	18, 4	150	25
114	19	154	25, 8
118	19, 8	158	26, 4
122	20, 4	162	27
126	21	166	27, 8
130	21, 8	170	28, 4
134	22, 4	174	29
138	23	178	29, 8
142	23, 8	182	30, 4
146	24, 4	186	31

(This guideline was first used by the RV Consumers Group.)

Remember, the length given in this chart is from the coupler to the rear axle of the trailer. It is not the total length of the trailer as in the previous chart.

When you're preparing to tow 3,500 to 7,000 pounds, your axle ratio should allow you the proper cruising range. For example, if you read the owner's manual for a current Ford truck, you'll see that the 7.3-liter diesel is only offered with 3.55, 4.10, or 5.13 axle ratios. The maximum GCW goes from a low of 11,000 pounds for the 3.55 to a whopping 17,000 pounds for the 5.13. Even more dramatic figures result when *continued on page 52*

continued on page 52

A tow vehicle this large is most useful for a tag-along trailer.

If you have a rig like this, you likely spend a lot of time towing trailers and want to be comfortable.

This bed design allows you to use a gooseneck or a tag-along trailer. While you lose the bed space that other trucks might have, the versatility is well worth it.

continued from page 50

we look at lower-powered engines. Take the 4.9-liter engine: You're limited to a trailer of only about 1,000 pounds if you have the 2.73:1 axle. This number goes to 6,000 pounds if you use the 4.10:1 rear axle ratio. Spend a lot of time looking at the specifications provided by the manufacturer.

If you're buying a new vehicle and plan on lots of long-distance towing, carefully consider the ideal rear axle ratio. Do your own homework. Don't depend on sales people in the dealership for anything. Keep in mind that axle ratios that are good for towing can seriously compromise your fuel economy during daily use. At any given speed, the engine is turning faster with a lower (higher numerically) axle ratio. Like everything else in this world, you have to make a tradeoff.

In general, vehicles with axle ratios below about 3.3:1 should only be used for limited towing. If the vehicle was equipped with a trailer-towing package when new, chances are the axle ratio was in the range of 3.3 to 4.0.

OVERDRIVE

Overdrive (OD) is a feature that's been around for a while. Overdrive today refers to a combination of gearing inside a transmission or transaxle that results in the speed of the output shaft being greater than the speed of the input shaft, thus reducing engine rpm. Generally speaking, overdrive (OD) is the highest gear in the transmission. Most modern automatic transmissions have five or six different speeds, and both fifth and sixth gears are overdrive gears. Overdrive allows the engine to operate at a lower rpm for a given road speed, allowing the vehicle to realize better fuel efficiency and often quieter operation on the highway.

With older trucks, you'll find that the gear selector levers have a D position and an OD. If you have it in D, you're limited to low, second, and high gears. In other words, you have a three-speed transmission. If you place the selector lever in OD, you effectively have a four-speed transmission. Some vehicles (such as Ford trucks) even have a push switch on the end of the selector lever that prevents or allows OD engagement.

If you check your owner's manual, you'll probably find a recommendation to either avoid or minimize the use of overdrive when towing. The reason for this is your transmission will automatically downshift to a lower gear when you either start to pull an increased load on the engine or force it by going to wide-open throttle.

Freightliner equips its bigger trucks with several storage areas, such as this one with automatic lighting and a door that stays open.

FACTORY TOW PACKAGE

Trailer packages vary by both truck brand and model, but here are some components that may be included. Towing packages have become increasingly complex in the last decade. In many cases the towing package even includes a different computer program for the operation of the transmission. Various manufacturers have somewhat different specifications, so you really need to check the manufacturer's websites to see what's actually part of the towing package. The only way to know for sure is to check the factory specifications.

- Hitch receiver
- Four- and/or seven-pin connector
- Larger alternator
- Larger battery
- Larger radiator
- Additional electric fan(s)
- Transmission fluid cooler
- Engine oil cooler
- Rear antisway bar
- Extendible mirrors
- Vehicle dynamic control
- Integrated brake controller
- Brake controller prewire
- Synthetic lubricants
- Lower axle ratio
- Re-valved shock absorbers

Older transmissions, such as those from the 1980s, often switch between OD and high as you climb shallow grades or slow down slightly in traffic. The transmission actually hunts around to find which gear is going to be the best ratio.

You might be pulling too heavy an engine load unless you either move the lever or put your foot into it to force a downshift, meaning you would have to develop a certain feel for towing a trailer.

All of this is changing very rapidly, though. Five- and six-speed transmissions are becoming very common. And the newer transmissions are getting really smart, too, with increasingly sophisticated computer controls.

Let's look at the recent BMWs, for instance, since I use one for towing. BMW has two types of six-speed automatics. One is a high-torque version, and the other is a low-torque version. There are actually 13 separate functions in this transmission. There are adaptive systems that respond to both your driving style and what you are actually doing with the vehicle. This adaptation system is reset each time you pull away from a standing stop. The system works by comparing inputs with a set of threshold values that were constructed from the time the SUV was last driven. The really interesting thing is that part of the BMW tow package is a transmission reprogram.

General Motors has recently started using what it calls a tow/haul mode. Chevy Silverado and GMC Sierra pickups delay the upshifts for improved towing and hauling. The higher upshift speeds and firmer gear changes are due to an increase in line pressure. This feature will not only give

A daily driver pulled behind a monster motorhome is called a dinghy.

you more control and durability of engine and transmission components but may even improve your fuel economy.

Recently, Ford has developed a similar feature that uses an adaptive learning strategy. This simply means the transmission knows you're carrying a load or towing a trailer and adjusts the transmission's shifting schedule accordingly. In this world of ever-advancing technology, what you learned 10 minutes ago may no longer be correct. Do your homework.

TOWING WITH A MOTORHOME

The equipment used to tow a small car or truck behind a motorhome doesn't need extensive maintenance. Simply grease the hitch ball if you're using a tow bar. If you use a tow dolly, then the wheel bearings should be repacked every year. If you happen to have a dolly with brakes, the brakes should be inspected annually.

Most important, use a proper combination of vehicles. A variety of compact cars, sport-utility vehicles, and trucks, including those with front-wheel drive and power steering, are approved by their manufacturers to be towed over long distances without speed restrictions.

To determine whether a vehicle is suitable to be towed behind a motorhome, check the owner's manuals of the models you are considering. If it's approved for towing, the owner's manual will have specific written instructions on how to tow it behind a motorhome. You may also want to visit a large RV store. The staff there can tell you right away if the combination you're considering makes good sense.

Most cars and trucks that aren't approved for towing on all four wheels can still be towed using aftermarket accessories, such as a cable-operated, driveshaft-disconnect device (rear-wheel-drive vehicles only), a driveshaft-disconnect device, free-wheeling hubs (front-wheel drive), a dolly, or a trailer.

Towing Options

There are three ways to tow a car behind a motorhome, and you need to decide which option best suits your needs.

Trailers

The first option is to simply use a trailer that allows you to raise all four wheels of your towed vehicle off the ground. These are most often used for sports cars or classic cars. All of the usual trailer requirements apply here. Just treat the trailer like you would any other trailer.

Be aware that most RV parks don't have room to let you park a trailer on your site along with your motorhome and trailered vehicle. Instead of one site for your motorhome, you'll need three parking places. In most cases, you'll have to unhook the trailer and park it somewhere away from your RV site.

Tow Dollies

A tow dolly is, essentially, a two-wheel, single-axle device that supports the front wheels of a car so that it can be towed and maneuvered in the same manner as a trailer. A dolly is recommended for front-wheel-drive vehicles because it lifts the front wheels of your vehicle off the pavement. When you put a front-wheel-drive vehicle on a dolly, you don't have to worry about the transmission or drivetrain rotating.

A tow dolly is also a great option if you intend to use it with multiple vehicles or want to share it with friends. Once you have a tow dolly, you might end up with a lot more friends.

Tow Bars

The most popular choice is to tow with all four wheels down using a tow bar. Tow bars are convenient and require the least amount of equipment to tow a vehicle. With a tow bar, you can unhook the car or truck and simply fold up the towing equipment. Since you don't have an actual trailer, you won't have to rent an additional parking space. A tow bar is also

TOW BAR SAFETY CHECKLIST

- Inspect the tow bar, dolly, or trailer for loose bolts and worn parts.
- Tighten loose bolts and replace worn parts before hooking up.
- Use Loctite on all bolts and nuts to keep them tight.

During Hookup

- Always hook up on a flat, smooth surface.
- If you have a coupler-style tow bar, check the fit of the coupler on the ball. Adjust the coupler if necessary.
- Hook up the tow bar.
- Set up the towed vehicle's steering and transmission for towing.
- Check the towed vehicle's parking brake and make sure it's disengaged.
- Latch the legs on a self-aligning tow bar.
- Attach the safety cables. Cross the cables between the vehicles, and wrap the cables around the tow bar legs to keep them from dragging.
- Attach the electrical cable.
- Check the operation of all the lights on both vehicles.
- Make sure you have a spare key, and lock the towed vehicle's doors.
- Always remember that your vehicle will be about 25 feet longer while towing.

During Towing

Each time you stop, check the tow bar, baseplate, and cables to make sure they're still properly attached. Always check the tires of the towed vehicle to make sure they're not going flat. If you're using a dolly or trailer, check the wheels to make sure they're not hot to the touch. If the wheels are hot, it could indicate a brake or bearing problem. Check the lights to make sure they're working properly. Between trips, take some time to clean the tow bar and cables to keep them in good shape. Also, clean and lubricate the tow bar as recommended by the manufacturer's instructions.

lighter to carry than a dolly or trailer, and prices for a tow bar start out lower than either a dolly or a trailer.

There are three general types of tow bars available: self-aligning car-mounted, self-aligning motorhome-mounted, and rigid A-frame. Before you select a tow bar, dolly, or trailer, check on the support that will be available as you travel across the country. Smaller companies do not have the dealer network or ability to help you after the sale.

Self-Aligning

A self-aligning tow bar enables you to hook up by yourself. The self-aligning feature allows you to drive up close to the tow vehicle and adjust the tow bar to the vehicle's position. The tow bar then extends out to its rigid tow position as you pull ahead with the tow vehicle. You can choose between car-mounted and motorhome-mounted units.

Car-mounted: Car-mounted, self-aligning tow bars were the first folding, self-aligning tow bars built. They were the industry standard for several years. When you're not towing with these tow bars, they fold and remain on the front of your car. Most models also have a quick-release system so they can be taken off quickly and easily.

Perhaps the biggest disadvantage to this type of tow bar is its appearance. Most people don't want to lift the weight of these tow bars, so they simply leave them on the car, which takes away from the look of your vehicle. In addition, leaving the extra weight of the tow bar on the front of the car affects the front suspension, especially with the really small cars that some people tow behind their motorhomes.

Motorhome-mounted: Motorhome-mounted, self-aligning tow bars are a popular new development. The main advantage of a motorhome-mounted tow bar is the replacement of the ball coupler with a swivel joint, which allows the tow bar to be used without a drop ball mount. In many cases, a drop ball mount hangs low enough to drag when the motorhome drives through a dip or starts up a ramp.

The storage of the tow bar on the motorhome leaves the front of the towed vehicle looking much nicer when you're not towing it. Also, the motorhome is less likely to be left in a place where theft is a major problem, and the tow bar can be locked into the receiver hitch of the motorhome to deter theft. This type of tow bar is also lighter and easier to handle than its car-mounted counterpart.

Rigid A-Frame

A rigid A-frame tow bar is simply a solid, welded tow bar without any adjustment to aid you in hooking it up. To hook up, you have to drive the towed vehicle to the exact spot that will allow you to put the tow bar's coupler on the ball of the tow vehicle. Hooking up a rigid A-frame tow bar is a two-person job: one person drives while the other person holds the tow bar up and guides the driver.

Rigid tow bars are the least expensive and generally some of the lightest tow bars you can buy. If you have a driver you can trust and one that can help without getting upset each time you hook up, the rigid A-frame may be an option for you. Also, if you only tow a vehicle once or twice a year, this may be the type of tow bar for your situation. Rigid tow bars normally have to be removed from the car and stored when not in use.

A small tow dolly allows you to tow a car occasionally. It is small, inexpensive, and easy to store when not in use. Most trailer stores rent tow dollies.

Baseplates

When you start to think about a dinghy towing system for your motorhome, don't overlook the baseplate. The baseplate is actually the bracket that bolts to the frame of your car (or dinghy, if you like); and it is custom designed for each specific car. (In other words, a Saturn baseplate won't fit on a Honda.)

Keep in mind that the steel of the baseplate will add more than 40 pounds to the vehicle's front axle since this baseplate is attached to the front of your dinghy. Some baseplates have tow-bar attachment tabs that can be removed when you're not towing. This looks a lot nicer and makes the front of your car look almost original. Some baseplates only leave a protruding electrical connector visible when everything is unhitched.

Choosing the correct baseplate, or bracket, tow bar, safety cables, and all the other associated accessories for your specific application is important. Even more important is that just because someone made a baseplate for your car doesn't mean you should tow it with all four wheels down. You really need to check your owner's manual for your car before you purchase a baseplate kit. You may need a new car in addition to a baseplate.

When you start shopping for a baseplate kit, make sure that you get one with all of the necessary hardware. Some of the kits require welding, and some require cutting the front panel on your car. Some require that you drill holes in the

frame of your car. Make sure you check all of this out before you hand over your Visa card.

While most of the baseplates can be installed in your driveway with a modicum of skill, I still prefer having a motorhome shop do it. You might do three installations in your lifetime. The motorhome shop might do three in one day. This is one case where it's worth paying someone to do the work. Besides, all that steel gets heavy when you are working with it in your driveway.

Most installation experts feel that the receiver hitch of the motorhome should never be more than 4 inches higher than the baseplate attachment points. Four inches or less keeps the tow bar level with the ground or slightly angled up toward the coach from the car. The tow bar should never be angled up toward the car from the coach.

You should visually inspect this baseplate on a regular basis. Make sure that the pins attaching the tow bar to the baseplate are in good condition. Pull them out, feel the surface to make sure they're not wearing. Check the operation of the retainer pins that hold the main pins in place. Make sure these pins still have resistance when you snap them in place to secure them. Don't forget to check the 5/8-inch pins that hold the tow bar to the motorhome receiver hitch. Replacement parts are cheap and you should replace any of these pins if worn. The general rule is, if you have any doubts about the parts just replace them.

Accessories

Your local RV store can provide all of the accessories that you may need or want for towing. For safety purposes, federal law requires motorhome-activated taillights and safety cables. Also, most U.S. states and Canadian provinces have laws requiring brakes for trailers (including towed cars). Brakes are required on trailers with GVWRs as low as 1,000 pounds in some states. These laws are not often enforced in the United States, most likely due to interpretation of the law's application to cars in tow.

British Columbia provincial authorities actively enforce trailer brake laws, stopping people, writing tickets, and making them drive the towed vehicle separately if they don't have the proper equipment. Remember that auxiliary braking systems are just that—auxiliary brakes. They are not meant to stop your motorhome any faster. They are designed to assist in slowing down the towed vehicle and to reduce the stopping distance that was changed due to the additional weight of the towed car.

Some Towing Issues

Some front-wheel-drive manual-transmission cars can be towed with all four wheels on the ground without modification. Most front-wheel-drive automatic-transmission vehicles will need a lube pump or similar device in order to tow them four wheels down. Rear-wheel-drive automatics will require a device to disconnect the driveshaft in order to tow with four wheels down. Some four-wheel-drive vehicles (both automatic and manual transmission) can also be towed. Refer to your owner's manual for specific instructions and limitations. Another great source of information about towing vehicles behind a motorhome is any large RV store that deals with motorhomes on a regular basis.

CHAPTER 4
IMPORTANT THINGS TO CONSIDER WHEN PURCHASING A TRAILER

Walking into the local trailer store can be overwhelming. The salespeople roll off a list of features that sets your head spinning. Before you even think about writing the check for your new trailer, slow down and think about the essentials. Forget the fancy pinstriping and LED lights. Instead, focus on strength, stability, and versatility.

TRAILER STRENGTH

Trailer strength is the first and the most important aspect of trailer design, no matter what size trailer you have. Strength is just as crucial with small utility trailers as it is with huge, 12,000-pound-capacity, tri-axle trailers. Strength may even be more important with small trailers, since they are frequently overloaded or loaded unevenly. By nature, small trailers are intended for utility. It's critical that they are strong and rigid to serve a variety of tasks.

I'm never sure about the welded versus bolted debate. I've seen too many trailers that are poorly bolted together. Properly used, bolts can be effective and efficient, especially with options that you may choose to add to your trailer.

Bolts must be secured to prevent them from vibrating loose (using lock nuts, for example). Many manufacturers use anaerobic sealers to keep things from vibrating apart, although the trailer industry prefers to use lock washers. If you take anything apart on your trailer, secure it back in place with a product such as Loctite, which is a readily available anaerobic sealer. These anaerobic sealers harden in the absence of air. When you tighten the bolt down, the sealer starts to harden, holding things in place. It takes about five minutes for this sealer to harden. Remember, the bolt and nuts threads must be absolutely clean for sealers such as Loctite to work properly.

If you're considering a trailer that's been bolted together, examine all of the bolted joints and make sure you're comfortable with the size and number of bolts. Also, look for lock nuts or other retainers to keep things tight. Finally, check to see what types of bolts are being used. You don't really need Grade 8 hardware. Grade 5 is safe and strong.

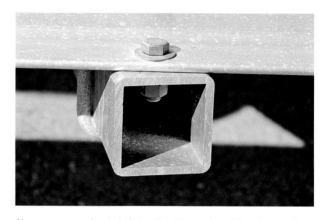

Always use a washer to bolt together the receiver. Otherwise, road vibrations could loosen the bolts—with undesirable results. Notice the clean cut on the aluminum stock.

The trailer's strength comes from one of two places: its frame or its sides. Light-duty trailers tend to have very light frames and rely on their sides for stiffness. Typically, these light utility trailers are made from angle iron, and the sides are welded angle iron, or tubing, that runs about a foot off the bed. A trailer that depends on its sides for stiffness is usually stiff and certainly light, but if you damage a side, the integrity of the entire trailer is compromised. Look closely at the design of the specific trailer you're considering to determine if it will be strong enough for your use.

If you're considering a welded trailer, check all of the welded joints to ensure that the welds are sufficient for the application. This inspection is subjective, but small short welds may indicate weakness or cheapness. A weld that runs the full length of a joint is obviously stronger than a series of spot welds.

Many trailers use gussets—metal plates added in the corners—for additional strength. Gussets greatly enhance the strength and rigidity of the trailer and allow smaller frame members to be used, which can save some weight. Ensure the gussets are welded along the entire edge, not just spot welded in place.

The coupler is welded into place on the trailer tongue. The chrome piece on the front of the coupler is a locking device to keep trailer thieves at bay.

Take the time to check for reinforcement, or additional material, in the areas where the axle springs mount. The points where the springs attach to the frame are the highest-stress points on the trailer. These points should be strong enough to handle any load you might put on or in the trailer.

Whether you're looking at an old or new trailer, a quick and dirty test of construction is to hook up the trailer and then jump up and down on each corner. The trailer should move up and down with you, but the frame shouldn't notice-ably twist. If twisting is noticeable, the design is weak. If one person jumping up and down on the trailer causes flexing, you don't want that trailer.

Examine the main load-carrying members and consider their size and thickness relative to the load capacity and the things you wish to carry. If a trailer looks cheap and cheesy, it probably is. Take a look at the flooring materials and the spacing between flooring support members. If you only intend to carry evenly distributed loads, the floor needs less strength than if your primary use will be to carry motorcycles, a race car, a horse, or anything where the weight is concentrated at just a few points. With cars and horses, all of the weight is concentrated on four points on the floor. Check that the floor is properly supported under the points where the weight will be located.

The strength of the crossmembers is critical. Even if the trailer is new, crawl underneath and look at the main beams and crossmembers for rust. Excessive rust will reduce capacity and is a sign of the care that went into the construction. Surface rust indicates a lack of care or shortcuts in finishing after construction. If the manufacturer skipped on using quality paint, where else did they cut corners?

The basic layout will have a tremendous effect on the stability of the trailer as you go down the road and can be a good indication of strength. The crossmembers used in the floor of the trailer are critical for overall strength and are easy to evaluate. The best flat-floor trailers have these cross-members placed at intervals of at least 16 inches. Some of the

The rear ramp brackets on this brand-new trailer are anything but straight: a definite red flag in terms of judging build quality. Inspect the trailer thoroughly before writing your check.

better horse trailers have crossmembers on 12-inch centers. While you're under the trailer, check to see if the longitudinal frame members are all one-piece items or if they are shorter lengths that have been spliced together.

What are the crossmembers constructed of? Some manufacturers use 3-inch channel, while others use 3-inch I-beams. Some manufacturers don't even use crossmembers; they simply place extruded aluminum planking crosswise on the trailer. Because it's really difficult to compare all the variations, I suggest that you visit at least a half-dozen trailer stores before buying a new trailer.

Tongue Length

The trailer's tongue should be long enough to allow a rea-sonable turning radius and clearance when backing. If the tongue is short, it may indicate shortcuts in the design. Short tongues affect drivability, turning radius, jackknife suscep-tibility, and stability, especially when backing up. A longer tongue extends the separation between the rear tires of the tow vehicle and the front axle of the trailer. The greater this

The bolted plate on top of the frame rails adds a great deal of rigidity. Also notice the Nylock nuts used to bolt the frame rails together.

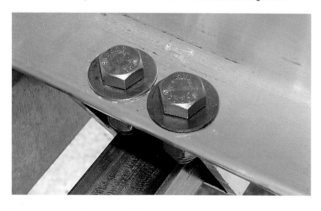

These large washers spread the stress and ensure greater long-term strength.

With washers and Nylock nuts, a quality trailer that's bolted together can be just as strong as a welded trailer.

The tongue on this trailer is very short. A longer tongue extends the distance between the tow truck's rear wheels and the front wheels on the trailer. Increasing this distance greatly improves the stability of the trailer.

distance, the greater the stability of the trailer as you tow it down the road.

The tongue should be totally integrated into the trailer frame so that the tongue and frame function as one unit. Thus, the trailer frame and trailer tongue should be made out of the same material.

Rear Crossmember

The rear frame crossmember of the trailer has to be really strong. Almost all of the loading and unloading occurs over the rear, so this crossmember should be larger than the others. This is also your rear bumper, so if there's ever a wreck, it needs to be strong.

Materials

Be sure that the materials and construction techniques used are adequate for your intended use. It's hard to make a visual judgment, but think about the size and relative strength of the materials and consider their effect on the overall strength. There's always a trade-off between strength and weight, so think about which way the designers of this trailer went. Most trailers will carry their specified load, but if that weight isn't distributed evenly, you can seriously damage the trailer.

Steel versus Aluminum Construction

Aluminum is a popular material for lightweight trailers. It can have an expensive look and feel. Aluminum can be used to make a very nice-looking trailer, but an aluminum trailer is always more expensive to build than a steel trailer. Pound for pound and foot for foot, aluminum costs more than steel. That means you'll pay a premium for an aluminum trailer. Are the benefits worth that extra money?

This massive trailer is set on a steel frame. The tongue of the trailer is huge, but the coupler ball appears to be undersized.

Generally, an aluminum trailer will last longer than a steel trailer, especially if you have a boat trailer that gets immersed in salt water on a regular basis. The same is true for horse and livestock trailers, where the ammonia in animal urine can wreak havoc on steel coatings.

Because aluminum is not as strong as steel, the beams of an aluminum trailer must be larger than steel beams would be for an equivalent capacity. Thus, the weight difference between an aluminum trailer and a steel trailer of equal strength may not be as large as you think. Given equivalent strength, an aluminum trailer will generally be lighter than a steel trailer, but the difference may be minimal.

Steel is extremely strong, but it yields to stress over time. New steel trailers are usually galvanized at the plant before they're painted. Ask questions about the manufacturer's galvanizing process. With a galvanized dip and epoxy paint, a steel trailer should hold up just as well as an aluminum trailer. If you are undecided about having a steel or aluminum frame under your trailer, think about what's used in your tow vehicle. There's a reason most trucks are made out of steel. The choice between aluminum and steel construction is never an easy one.

Hybrids

Steel and aluminum hybrids are rapidly becoming the trailers of choice. Steel is usually used for the frame of the trailer,

and some combination of fiberglass and aluminum is used for the areas that receive little stress. With this design, weight can be kept to a reasonable level without sacrificing structural integrity. In addition, the price can be kept below that of an all-aluminum trailer.

Many aluminum boat trailers use a galvanized steel crossmember to hold the trailer together. When something absolutely has to hold the trailer, most companies rely on steel. The days of all-steel and all-aluminum trailers may well be over.

TRAILER STABILITY

Poor load distribution is the most common cause of instability. Fortunately, it's also the easiest problem to correct. The trailer load should be distributed from side to side with at least 10 percent of the trailer weight on the hitch. With typical trailers, slightly more weight (up to 15 percent of the trailer weight) on the hitch is better for stability.

When you have too much weight resting on the hitch in the rear of the tow vehicle, the front of the vehicle can rise. With too much weight on the hitch, you'll have stability, drivability, and control problems, because weight is lifted off the steering wheels. To correct this problem, load-distributing hitches can be used to level the trailer with respect to the tow vehicle. These hitches can make a big difference, especially when trailer size and/or weight are near, or exceed, that of the

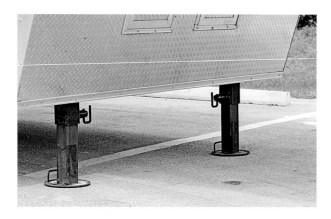

If you have a big trailer it only stands to reason that you need massive stabilizer units. Both of these units have a large footprint that will keep them from sinking into the pavement.

This 48-foot-long trailer can easily hold two race cars.

A trailer this tall will be subject to even the smallest side winds, but you can place a lot of very tall things in it. For instance, you may tow one car above another in order to have a shorter trailer. There is a tradeoff between length and height.

tow vehicle. A trailer that is properly configured and loaded shouldn't need a damper, although in a pinch, it can help to correct trailer stability issues. (A damper is essentially a shock absorber used between the trailer and the tow vehicle.)

The trailer's axle should be located behind the center of the load for stability. Many trailers have the axle at, or just barely behind, the center of the trailer bed. This setup assumes that the load will be heaviest at the front. This assumption is shortsighted with respect to versatility, and it's also an indication of weakness. For most applications, the axle should be behind the center of the bed. The ultimate arrangement for maximum versatility would allow the axle position to be adjusted. On the average single-axle utility trailer, roughly 60 percent of the trailer bed should be in front of the axle.

Trailer length—especially length with respect to the width of the trailer—is a huge factor in stability. Longer trailers typically tow better. A greater separation between the rear wheels of the tow vehicle and the forward wheels of the trailer will always enhance stability. A long tongue can also help in facilitating this separation. Most trailer manufacturers

will allow you to select the length of the tongue. A longer tongue will give you more stability, but it could create storage problems for you.

A long distance between the location of the hitch point and the rear wheels of the tow vehicle will negatively affect stability. When this distance is shorter, the trailer doesn't wag the tow vehicle as much, and the bumps of the tow vehicle don't affect the trailer as much. For example, fifth-wheel trailers are easy to tow because the hitch is almost directly above the rear axle of the truck. The opposite is true when there is a long overhang (when using a school bus for towing, for instance).

Brakes can greatly affect trailer stability. The brakes— both electric and surge—need to be calibrated and applied appropriately for the load, trailer size, and tow vehicle. (For more information on brakes, see Chapter 7.)

Dynamic loads, or loads that move around, can have a significant effect on stability. For instance, if a large, heavy pipe isn't tied down, it'll roll from side to side or front to back with the motion of the trailer. This constantly changing load makes the trailer move. If the dynamic load is small compared to the weight of the trailer, the effect may not be

The fixed sides limit the use of this trailer.

important; but if the moving load is large, the effect can be quite significant. Animals in tow can also have this effect. In general, the load should be secured as much as possible to accommodate stability.

Center of gravity is another important consideration. In general, a lower center of gravity helps stability. This rule is especially true with boat trailers; the heavy hull should be as close to the road as possible. The same is true of car trailers; lower deck height is always a good thing.

Aerodynamic effects caused by the load, side winds, or other vehicles can contribute to stability problems. Typically, larger trailers, such as campers and fifth-wheel trailers, suffer most from aerodynamic effect. Nonetheless, you have to be careful to load a utility trailer aerodynamically. Even minor things on the trailer, such as sharp corners, contribute to aerodynamic stability.

Along with aerodynamics, trailer attitude affects stability. Attitude is the relationship of the trailer with respect to the ground and the tow vehicle. Always strive to get the trailer level with the ground. Quite simply, you do not want the rear end of the trailer dragging on the ground, nor do you want the tongue sitting low. Your trailer should always be level.

There are a lot of items that affect the stability and safety of a trailer; all need some consideration, but a few are more

important. Items of construction include wheel and axle alignment, axle placement, brakes, calibration, and overall strength. Always consider trailer attitude with respect to the ground. Remember that tire condition (especially inflation pressure), and load distribution are critical to getting the

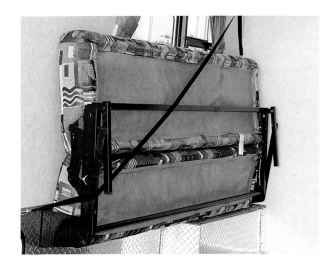

With the bed folded into the wall, you can fill the rear of the toy box trailer with motorcycles and ATVs.

This smaller toy box trailer, designed for an ATV or a couple of motorcycles, features a nonskid ramp. Since there are times you're going to have to load up in the rain, the nonskid surface can be a wonderful thing to have.

trailer level to the ground. By considering, adjusting, and correcting these things, your trailer will tow in a stable, predictable, and enjoyable manner.

TRAILER VERSATILITY

You should be able to use your trailer for more than one purpose. One of the best examples of versatility I've seen is a twin-axle trailer with sides that can be totally removed. This trailer is perfect for hauling a load of mulch home from the garden center one weekend and taking the race car to the drag strip the next weekend. Indeed, if I were ordering a utility trailer today, I would insist on removable sides, regardless of the size of the trailer.

Some of the new motorcycle trailers are really versatile. The channels for the motorcycle tires can be removed from the deck, leaving a perfect space for just about anything you might want to haul. I've even seen a motorcycle trailer with pockets around the edges for sidewalls. There's no real reason to buy a dedicated motorcycle trailer. Versatility is a critical factor in new trailer design.

The four U-bolts provide the winch post with great versatility. It's hard to imagine a boat that wouldn't fit here.

CHAPTER 5
BASIC TRAILER SUSPENSIONS

You probably haven't given much thought to the axle(s) under your trailer. The single most important thing you need to know about your axle is how much weight it can hold. Every axle is designed to hold a given amount of weight. If you load more weight onto your trailer than the axle(s) can hold, the result will not be pretty. Fortunately, if you bought a commercially produced trailer, the people who put the axle(s) under your trailer did the necessary calculations. If you're building your own trailer, pay close attention to this chapter.

SELECTING THE PROPER TRAILER AXLE

The following suspension information is only necessary if you're building or modifying a trailer. When your trailer comes from a major manufacturer, all of this has been figured out for you.

Load Capacity

The axle has to support the maximum gross vehicle weight rating (GVWR). For multiple-axle trailers, divide the GVWR by the number of axles to determine the load capacity of each axle. You would be wise to use axles that can support slightly more than the weight of the trailer and its load. A little fudge factor never hurts. In fact, most trailer companies have already done this for you.

Track Length

The easiest way to find your axle length, or track length, is to measure the distance between the center of one tire and the center of the opposite tire. This measurement varies depending on what type of wheel is used, because each type of wheel (White Spoke, OEM, custom) could have a different offset. This offset changes the distance between the center of

This trailer has an extra hole for the spring mount (on the far right of the picture). This allows the owner to change the location of the rear eye.

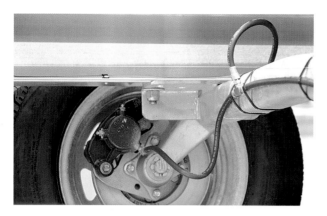

The torsion axle's compact size is one of the real advantages over a trailer with leaf springs.

With a tandem axle equalizer, or spring equalizer, the load is transferred from one spring to the other as you hit bumps on the road.

The Mor/ryde suspension is unique because it provides over 5 inches of suspension travel. Leaf springs typically provide 2 or 3 inches of travel. The Mor/ryde suspension system can be retrofitted to a fifth-wheel trailer.

the two tires. This effectively changes the track length. If you need to replace an axle, you're going to need a more accurate number than track length.

You can improve the accuracy of this measurement by measuring the distance from one hub face to the other hub face. The hub face is the mounting surface where the wheel studs

are located. It's a machined surface, so those measurements are much more accurate than a tire-to-tire measurement.

Overall Axle Length

The overall axle length is the distance from the very end of an axle's spindle to the very end of the opposite spindle. It isn't

Leaf springs are the suspension systems most commonly found on trailers. They generally work well and are inexpensive. Over time, however, the bushings wear out and need to be replaced.

This slipper-style end isn't commonly used on single-axle trailers, although some people feel it offers increased stability. Others feel this type of end makes too much noise and allows too much wear on the metal parts of the suspension.

an easy measurement to make, so it is seldom used. It can be a useful reference number, though, if you're shopping for axles or building your own trailer.

Spring Center

The distance from the center of one spring to the center of the spring on the opposite side is called the spring center. You can also think of this as the distance from one spring mounting pad on the axle to the spring mounting pad on the other side. Normally, the spring centers are matched to the frame width of the trailer. This information is useful if you have to replace the axle on your trailer.

Axle Style

Axle style is important if you're reusing old mounting hardware and also to ensure that you have proper tire clearance. The choices include straight axles (round or square), drop axles with offset spindles, and torsion axles. You should also consider spindle size if you intend to reuse your existing hubs or drums.

Camber

Some axles are cambered so there's a bow in the axle until weight is put on it. All cambered axles should be mounted with the center bow up. Because the weight of your load will actually straighten the axle, the camber is usually 1 degree or less. You may not even be able to see the positive camber since it's such a minimal number.

Bolt Pattern

The bolt pattern of the axles can vary depending on the capacity of the axle. The bolt pattern also determines what type of wheel can be used on your trailer. If you have six lug nuts you obviously can't use a wheel that has only five holes. The thing you might forget is that the more lug nuts used on an axle, the stronger that axle will be.

SUSPENSION RECOMMENDATIONS

Axle Clearance

Leaf spring axles need clearance from the frame to operate properly. If the spring hangers are too short, the axle could contact the frame during movement of the suspension and result in overloading the axle and possible damage. If the spring hangers are too long and provide too much clearance, the springs could be damaged if excessive loads are placed on the trailer and the axle moves too much. If this condition exists, use bump stops to prevent overtravel.

Each suspension type has advantages and disadvantages. Suspension options are sometimes overlooked because leaf springs with pivots are so common. Slipper-type leaf springs are especially popular on high-capacity and multi-axle trailers. Rubber torsion suspensions are gaining popularity on light-duty trailers because of their compactness. When considering suspension, there are a few things to think about. The key is to use the right suspension for the application. You can have multiple axles, straight axles, dropped axles, leaf springs, torsion bars, and, in some cases, even coil springs. The choices are almost limitless.

Types of Leaf Springs

The leaf spring is by far the most common trailer suspension system, so we'll talk about that first. There are three basic types of springs to choose from.

Single-Axle Leaf Springs

The leaf spring with dual eyes for mounting is far and away the first choice for most single-axle trailers. Trailers with dual-eye leaf springs are easy to use because they're light-weight. A single-axle trailer is really as much trailer as most people need. Single-axle trailers are also more efficient to pull and allow for better fuel mileage. Here are some key points to consider:

- **Advantages:** Single-axle applications are less expensive than dual-axle trailers, require far less maintenance, and are easier to maneuver. Single-axle trailers minimize stress on the frame because they apply a simple vertical load at four points on the frame. A single-axle trailer is easy to set up, so the axle position is usually correct.
- **Disadvantages:** Single-axle leaf springs can take up a lot of room under the trailer and limit how close the bed can be to the ground. This limitation is especially true if the axle is located below the leaf spring. The bed will be high, and

Slipper-style leaf springs come in a variety of different ends. A radius end is shown here.

the loads you carry will be equally high. Remember, a high center of gravity is not a good thing for towing.

Multiple-Axle Leaf Springs

If you double or triple the number of axles on your trailer, you will double or triple the number of springs you use.

- **Advantages:** Multiple leaf springs distribute a simple load fairly well to several different points on the frame. They can be designed to share the load with a rocker link between the two leaf springs.
- **Disadvantages:** Multiple leaf springs take up a lot of space and pose serious limitations on bed height. Different variations on multiple leaf springs exist, but the load sharing for the rear axle is typically not as well constrained as the front, so these trailers tend to be less stable than a simple single-axle trailer.

Multiple axles should be used when loads are large or too heavy for a standard single axle. Multiple axles are also appropriate when the trailer is quite long. However, it's usually cheaper and easier to strengthen a long frame than to add axles. The weight of the load becomes the controlling factor.

Slipper-Style Leaf Springs

If you have a really heavy boat or a race car to haul around, you might consider slipper-style leaf springs. One end of this leaf spring has a traditional eye, and the other end slides in a keeper, or hanger, that is welded to the trailer frame. This design provides a lot more stability.

- **Advantages:** Slipper-style leaf springs offer some packaging advantages, but not a great deal. They are not often used on single-axle trailers because they don't have many advantages over the pivot style. For multiple-axle trailers, slipper-style leaf springs make mounting and load distribution much easier—particularly with three or more

The equalizer gets a lot of use and abuse. If the wear is severe, you can replace the bushings or the equalizer itself. Check for cracks periodically.

The pivot arm on the torsion axle moves up and down as the wheel encounters bumps in the road.

axles. In multiple-axle applications, especially for high capacity, these leaf springs are very popular. They share the load well and provide stability.

- **Disadvantages:** Slipper-style leaf spring systems can be noisy on rough roads, because there is a loose spring end that can move around. They can also create a lot of wear on the metal parts that rub together.

Torsion Axles

Torsion axles are the hot ticket these days. They have some huge advantages and only a few limitations. A torsion-axle suspension has a lower profile, so the trailer rides closer to the ground. Torsion bars are a very good choice if you want a low bed with enhanced loaded stability. Loading the trailer is also easier since the trailer bed is lower. Even better, if the

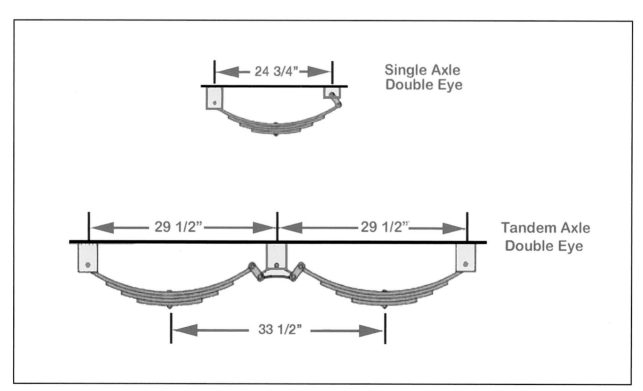

Single Axle
Double Eye
← 24 3/4" →

Tandem Axle
Double Eye
← 29 1/2" → ← 29 1/2" →
← 33 1/2" →

You can measure your springs before you remove them by simply measuring the distance between the shackle bolts on the chassis. If you have a dual-axle trailer, measure from the center of the equalizer to the shackle bolt.

Every 10 years or so, remove the springs and replace the bushing in the eyelet and the bolt that holds everything together.

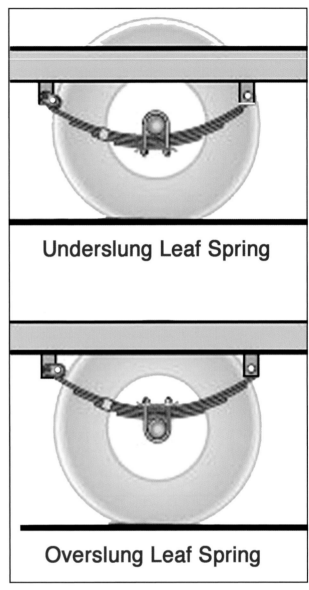

Underslung Leaf Spring

Overslung Leaf Spring

The location of the spring on the axle can make a big difference in the deck height of your trailer. The two basic choices, underslung and overslung, are shown here.

suspension fails, the axle can't detach itself from the trailer bed. When you break a leaf spring, or even a spring shackle, it can be dangerous.

The wheel/hub spindle attaches to a lever, called the torsion arm, which is fastened to a rubber-encased bar. As load is applied, the bar rotates, causing a rolling/compressive resistance in the rubber cords, or bar. This action provides the same function as a conventional sprung axle.

In the unlikely event that the suspension fails, the torsion axle can't detach from the trailer bed. Such detachment can happen when a spring breaks on a standard trailer suspension. Suspension failure may never happen to you, but if it does, you'll quickly realize one huge advantage of the torsion axle.

In addition, each wheel on a torsion-axle trailer can move independent of the others. In a leaf spring setup, the shock absorption is achieved by several flat pieces of metal that are arched. When the trailer encounters a bump in the road, the springs bend in the opposite direction but return to their arched shape. Because leaf springs are connected with a solid axle, movement on one side of the trailer is transmitted to the other side; some engineers call this "cross-talk." When the right side of the trailer hits a bump, that movement will be transmitted to the left side. With leaf springs, movement is constantly transmitted from one side of the trailer to the other. That doesn't happen with torsion axles.

When properly loaded, both leaf springs and torsion suspension systems will handle the same amount of weight but may have different ride characteristics. Anecdotally, most people feel the torsion suspension gives a softer ride.

Every six months to one year, check the mounting bolts to make sure everything is secure. Aside from that checkup, torsion-axle suspensions require no maintenance.

Most spring shackles contain bushings that wear out after a few years.

- **Advantages:** Torsion bars can be very compact and allow significant freedom in designing a trailer. The elasticity of the torsion bar also provides natural damping to the bumps in the road. Because they are single-sided units, torsion bars create a truly independent suspension. Torsion axles are a good choice for light-duty trailers.
- **Disadvantages:** One consideration with a torsion-axle suspension system is that all of the forces are localized on a very specific point on the frame. Some people feel that this adds significant stress compared to simple leaf springs. That's why some people with really heavy trailers stay away from torsion axles. They just feel more comfortable with the traditional leaf springs. Second, the load distribution to the frame can be complex, especially when individual units are used, creating forces in two directions. Third, torsion bars don't load share in multiple-axle configurations. Thus, as a trailer is pulled over a bump, one axle takes far more of the load than the other. That means one side could overload while the other is hardly loaded at all. Finally, because the spring is elastic, it has a limited life. Over several years, the torsion bar will gradually harden and its compliance (softness) will diminish. I happen to believe that by the time the torsion bar hardens, the frame of the trailer will also reach the end of its useful life.

Coil Springs

Coil springs are not very common on trailers because they require a lot of stuff to hold the axle in place. While coils springs can be the most compliant and can allow the most suspension travel, they require more complex attachment devices (such as trailing arms) and therefore use vertical space very inefficiently. The complexity and additional costs simply don't offset the advantages that might be found.

The same is true of transverse springs. They're not widely used because of their limitations. The biggest problem is that the trailer tends to sit too high off the ground.

Shock Absorbers

Most trailers don't have shock absorbers. In general, if you wish to have a cushioned ride, shocks are great. If a little bouncing doesn't bother the load, shocks are not necessary. (Shocks won't reduce the bouncing of an empty trailer. Shock absorbers work between the axle and the frame, but the bouncing of a nearly empty trailer is all in the tires. To avoid this bouncing, simply reduce tire pressure to around 10 psi when the trailer is empty. Just remember to return the tires to the normal pressure when you load the trailer.)

SUSPENSION MAINTENANCE

Suspension components do wear out, although very few people ever think about suspension maintenance. We spend so much time worrying about brakes and lights that we completely forget about the suspension.

Leaf Spring Bushings

The little rubber bushings that fit in the eyes of the leaf springs take a tremendous beating from normal use. Over time, these do deteriorate. Fortunately, they are easy and inexpensive to replace. However, if you have a large trailer, such as a fifth-wheel RV trailer, bushing replacement is better left to the professionals at a trailer dealership.

Replacing Your Leaf Springs

Springs do actually wear out. There are times when a leaf spring can actually break. If that happens, you have no choice but to replace the springs. If you get to the point of replacing leaf springs, you need to replace both sides. If you have a dual-axle trailer, replace all four springs to be on the safe side.

CHAPTER 6
TRAILER TIRES AND WHEELS

A trailer's tires and wheels should match the load capacity of the trailer, and they should be designed for trailer use. Even though passenger-car tires are commonly used on trailers, it is not a good idea. Be sure to use tires that are designed for trailer use.

Tires that are designed to be used on boat, car, or utility trailers are labeled with an "ST" (which stands for Special Trailer). ST tires should never be used on cars, vans, or light trucks. ST tires are constructed for better high-speed durability and bruise resistance under heavy loads. Trailer tire construction varies substantially from automotive tires; therefore, it's important to choose the right tire for your trailer. If you bought your trailer new and from a reputable trailer dealer, you're doing just fine. Those of us who buy used trailers have to pay close attention to this tire issue.

In general, trailer tires have the same load range, or ply rating, from bead to bead and are bias-ply construction. This design allows for a stiffer sidewall that provides safer towing by helping to reduce trailer sway. The use of passenger-car (P) or light-truck (LT) tires a on a trailer is a problem because these tires, whether radial or bias, have more flexible sidewalls. Flexible-sidewall tires on your trailer could lead to increased sway and loss of control.

Goodyear has published the following guidelines for ST tires. This is good information from the guys who make the tires. It would behoove you to pay attention.

- Industry standards dictate that tires with the ST designation are speed restricted to 65 miles per hour under normal inflation and load conditions, unless a different speed restriction is indicated on the sidewall of the tire.
- Based on industry standards, if tires with the ST designation are used at speeds between 66 and 75 miles per hour, it's necessary to increase the cold inflation pressures by 10 psi above the recommended pressure for the load.
- Don't exceed the maximum pressure for the wheel.
- If the maximum pressure for the wheel prohibits the increase of air pressure, then the maximum speed must be restricted to 65 miles per hour.

Setting the wheels wider can give the trailer more stability. In this case, the longer axle also provides more space inside the trailer. The plastic fenders alleviate water spray as you drive down the road.

This trailer uses bolts, rather than studs and lug nuts, to hold the wheel in place. The torque setting is usually different for bolts than for nuts.

In a perfect world, all six tires on this trailer should be the same size and the same brand, because tire diameters vary slightly from one company to the next.

ST175/80 D 13 is the size of the tire, and it's the equivalent of a B78-13 tire.

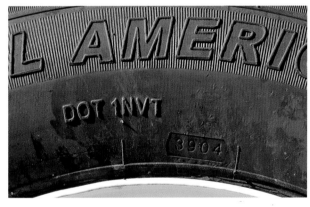

The DOT 1NVT marking indicates the factory that produced the tire and the mold batch. The 3904 means that the tire was produced in the 39th week of 2004.

- The cold inflation pressure must not exceed 10 psi beyond the inflation specified for the maximum load of the tire.

WHEEL SIZING

Traditionally, there are three critical areas to consider for wheels: diameter, offset, and bolt pattern. (A wheel described as a 14x5.5 wheel has a diameter of 14 inches and a width of 5.5 inches.)

Diameter

The wheel and tire diameter must be large enough to provide sufficient ground clearance when used with spindle-type axles. If you don't have enough clearance, you could have

This radial ST tire has an all-season designation.

axle components dragging on the ground in the case of a flat tire. Given all of the possible wheel problems, it is best to stick with the wheel diameter that the manufacturer used on your trailer.

Although I'm not a big fan of changing tire and wheel diameter on a trailer, I make two exceptions: Snowmobile trailers and trailers for personal watercraft can usually benefit from an increase in diameter. The same goes for some of the really small boat trailers. Generally, I don't like the 10-inch wheels that come with these types of trailers. Small tires run too hot on long expressway trips.

Offset

The offset of a wheel is the distance from the mounting surface of the wheel to the true centerline of the rim. A positive offset means the mounting surface of the wheel is positioned in front of the true centerline of the rim, which places the tire in toward the frame of the trailer. Conversely, a negative offset means the mounting surface of the wheel is behind the true centerline of the rim, which will cause the tire to stick out away from the trailer.

There's no real advantage, or disadvantage, to different offsets. It's just that if the trailer is designed for a certain amount of offset in one direction, you have to use wheels that are similar in the exchange. The wrong wheels could end up sticking out beyond the fenders, or rubbing against the trailer frame.

Keep in mind that your trailer was engineered as a total package. The only reason you might choose to change the wheels is to give your trailer some visual impact. However, there's no need to change the diameter. You'll get no real benefit by installing 18-inch or 20-inch automotive wheels, and you could create problems.

Bolt Pattern

The number of lug nuts gives you a rough guess as to the strength of the axle, and your axle determines what wheels to use. Lightweight trailers often have only four studs, which correspond to an axle that can generally handle up to 2,000 pounds. Axles that can handle 3,500 pounds usually have five or six lug nuts. When you get to axles that can handle 6,000 pounds or more, the wheels will have six or eight lug nuts.

The number of bolts and the diameter of the circle those bolts make up is called the bolt pattern. The bolt openings on the wheels are bored to perfectly match up with the bolt pattern on the axle.

There are two totally different types of wheels: hub-centric and lug-centric. With a hub-centric wheel, the center is very closely machined, meaning the weight of the trailer is actually carried by the hub of the wheel. The lug nuts are only used to fasten the wheel to the axle, not to carry the weight of the trailer. With a lug-centric wheel, the center hub hole is machined larger than necessary, allowing the wheel to fit a variety of applications. On a lug-centric wheel, the lug nuts support the weight of the trailer. In this less-than-ideal

The number of lug nuts is a good indication of wheel strength. This is clearly a strong wheel.

Ten-inch tires are cheaper than the larger sizes, but the larger sizes run cooler on long trips.

These strong wheels are commonly called "wide-fives" because of the way the lug nuts are located.

If you use closed lug nuts, make sure that they don't hit the stud. A lug nut that's too short could cause a serious problem.

These wheels were balanced at the factory, which indicates a higher level of quality.

Spoke steel wheels are the most popular trailer wheels, because they're strong and inexpensive.

This lug-centric wheel was properly installed. To do this, gently tighten the lug nuts and spin the wheel to see if it is properly centered. Then tighten the lugs nuts to the appropriate torque.

design, the studs are asked to do a great deal more than they were designed to. These cheaper lug-centric wheels are often used on less-expensive trailers.

When you tighten a lug-centric wheel, make sure that every lug nut is centered on its seat before you actually tighten down the wheel. You might think you have the wheel on properly, but it's really off center to the hub.

WHEEL AND TIRE SAFETY

If a wheel on your trailer is off center, you will have problems with stability, tracking, and safety. Every now and then, jack up your trailer and spin the tires, looking for wobble. The wobble may come from a bent rim or from a wheel that is not attached properly. And if the wheel doesn't spin freely, you probably have a bearing problem. Your day just got worse.

Tires should always be properly inflated. The ideal inflation pressure, however, will vary depending on conditions. When a trailer is to be pulled a long distance while empty or without a significant load, tire pressure can be reduced as much as 10 to 15 psi.

Keep in mind that the tires are really springs. The tires soak up the road inconsistencies and function as a damper to keep the trailer from bouncing around. When you change the pressure in the tires, you're actually changing the total spring rate of the trailer. More pressure is like having slightly stiffer springs. Lower tire pressures give you a slightly lower spring rate.

Remember that the load rating for your trailer is at a given tire pressure. When you go below that tire pressure, you're actually reducing the load capacity of the trailer. When the trailer is loaded, the inflation pressure should be increased per the tire manufacturer's recommendations.

LUG NUT TORQUE

The lug nut torque specification for trailers is usually much higher than that used on passenger-car wheels. Check your particular trailer's recommended specifications. Most require 90 to 95 ft-lb. After the first 25 to 50 miles of towing with a new trailer, check the torque on all wheels. Check them again at the first rest stop. After that, check the lug nuts every time you get ready for a road trip of any length.

On your car or truck, the wheels actually turn as you go around a corner. With a trailer, the wheels are fixed in place while turning. Thus, when you go around a corner, the trailer wheel flexes a lot more that the tow vehicle's wheels. This flex occurs because of the additional side forces that are placed on the trailer wheels.

Because of this flexing, lug nut torque on a trailer is more complicated than on a car. You can't simply tighten

⚠ NOTICE
- Check wheel lugs for tightness after 50 miles and frequently thereafter.
- Grease wheel bearings every 10,000 miles, or once a year. More frequently under abnormal conditions.

HAULMARK INDUSTRIES, INC.

HA2006

All trailer owners should follow these two practices.

OLDER LOAD RANGE DESIGNATIONS

Load Range B = old 4-ply rating
Load Range C = old 6-ply rating
Load Range D = old 8-ply rating

WHEEL TORQUE REQUIREMENTS

Axle Size (pounds)	Wheel Size (inches)	Stud Size (inches)	Steel Wheel Torque (ft-lb)	Aluminum Wheel Torque (ft-lb)
2,000	13	1/2	50–75	N/A
3,500	15	1/2	90–120	90–120
5,200	15	1/2	90–120	90–120
6,000	16	9/16	90–120	90–120
7,200	16	9/16	90–120	90–120
8,000	12–16.5	5/8	90–120	N/A

The strongest wheels on the market are made of forged aluminum like these.

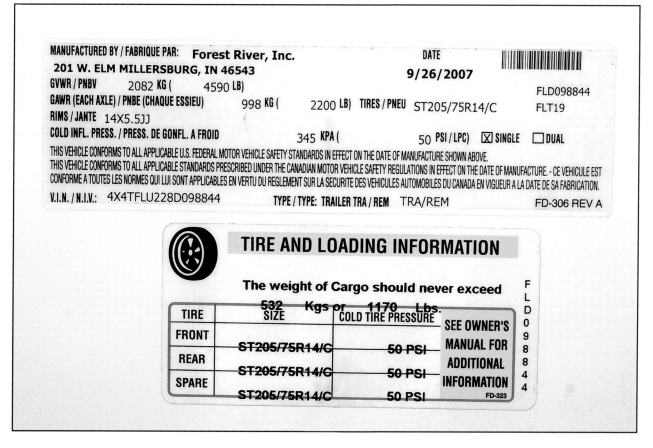

The trailer's load rating is calculated with 50 psi in the tires. If you allow the pressure to go below 50 psi, you'll seriously reduce the load capacity of this trailer.

the lug nuts with greater force, because that will stretch the bolts beyond their designed capacity. Instead, check the lug nuts several times during the first few hundred miles of use. Continue to check the torque until it stabilizes. Check the lug nut torque after 50, 150, and 300 miles. After that, it should be fine until the next time you remove the wheel. Then you will need to go through the same procedure until the lug nut torque again stabilizes at the required setting.

A lot of people keep a torque wrench with all of their towing gear. Get a 1/2-inch-drive wrench, the appropriate socket, and a 6-inch extension, and keep all of these items with the trailer.

ALUMINUM VERSUS STEEL WHEELS

There are three things to consider when looking at trailer wheels: strength, durability, and cost. With these things in mind, the decision between aluminum and steel wheels is simple. Most high-performance trailer wheels are made of an aluminum alloy, which offers several advantages. Alloy wheels look really nice and, when properly manufactured, they are really strong. Aluminum wheels are normally stronger than steel wheels of the same size.

TIRE LOAD CAPACITY INDEX

Load index	Pounds	Kilograms	Load index	Pounds	Kilograms
91	1,356	615	101	1,819	825
92	1,389	630	102	1,874	850
93	1,433	650	103	1,929	875
94	1,477	670	104	1,984	900
95	1,521	690	105	2,039	925
96	1,565	710	106	2,094	950
97	1,609	730	107	2,149	975
98	1,653	750	108	2,205	1,000
99	1,709	775	109	2,271	1,030
100	1,764	800	110	2,337	1,060

Top-quality aluminum wheels are also very round. Not all wheels are as round as they should be. A forged aluminum wheel that is machined in the final manufacturing stage is about as good as it gets. Round and balanced wheels will put

This tire is 8-ply rated and is certified as a Load Range D. Never ever put a tire on your trailer that is rated lower than the original tires that were installed at the factory.

At 50 psi, a Load Range C tire can carry 1,820 pounds of weight. Two of these tires on a single-axle trailer can only carry 3,600 pounds. If these tires are used on a dual-axle trailer, you can carry loads up to 7,200 pounds.

TIRE LOADS AT DIFFERENT PRESSURES

Running your trailer tires with low air pressure can seriously compromise the integrity of the tire. Low pressure dramatically lowers the amount of load that an ST tire can handle. The chart below is an example of how dramatic this difference can be. For tire pressure information for your specific brand, contact a tire store in your area.

Tire Size	Max Speed Rating (mph)	Inflation Pressure (psi)								
		15	20	25	30	35	40	45	50	55
ST175/80R13	65	670	795	905	1,000	1,100(B)	1,190	1,270	1,360(C)*	
ST185/80R13	65	740	870	990	1,100	1,200(B)	1,300	1,400	1,480(C)	
ST205/75R14	65	860	1,030	1,170	1,300	1,430(B)	1,530	1,640	1,760(C)	
ST215/75R14	65	953	1,110	1,270	1,410	1,520(B)	1,660	1,790	1,870(C)	
ST205/75R15	65	905	1,070	1,220	1,360	1,480(B)	1,610	1,720	1,820(C)	
ST225/75R15	65	1,060	1,260	1,430	1,600	1,760	1,880	2,020	2,150(C)	2,270
ST235/80R16	65	1,720	1,920	2,090	2,270	2,430	2,600	2,730	2,870	

*The letters in parentheses denote the load range at a given inflation.

a lot less stress on your tires. Beware of aluminum wheels from Chinese manufacturing facilities. These wheels are gravity cast with no thought given to quality. Gravity-cast aluminum wheels are the bottom-feeders in the wheel industry. I would not use a gravity-cast alloy trailer wheel. The Alcoa wheels common on high-end trailers are high-quality forged aluminum.

Remember that in most cases, a trailer wheel carries more weight than an automotive wheel. Thus, trailer wheels need to be stronger than automotive wheels. High-quality wheels are tested to meet industry standards for safety and quality. Original equipment manufacturers (OEMs) have to follow these industry standards. There are no standards for aftermarket wheels; you pay your money and take your chances.

In terms of durability, forged aluminum wheels are again superior to stamped steel wheels. Ask yourself whether forged aluminum wheels are worth the extra money. If you're only hauling light loads, you're probably better off with regular steel wheels.

Steel wheels are adequate for a low-capacity utility trailer used for hauling gardening supplies and other light loads. Since the stress on your trailer tires will be very low in this case, the aluminum alloy wheels are unnecessary.

If you think you might want to switch wheels on your trailer, keep in mind that most aluminum wheels are thicker in the mounting bolt area than a steel wheel. You'll oftentimes have to install longer studs to mount the aluminum wheels.

Also pay attention to the offset of the wheel. Most of the bearing sets used in trailer axles are designed for wheels with a 0- to 1/2-inch offset. If you put wheels with a different offset on your trailer, you'll put extra stress on the wheel bearings. The bearings will wear out faster and will need to be replaced more often.

There are several types of lug nuts available, and you must use the type designed for the wheel you're using. The

Wheel Masters has created a dual tire equalization tool that connects the inside and outside tires on your tow truck. The system of stainless-steel braided hoses keeps the pressure in the tow tires equalized.

bolt holes on the wheel have a certain taper, or cone angle, and your lug nuts must have the same taper.

LOAD RANGE

Tire load range (the maximum weight each tire can safely support) must be considered when selecting the proper tire size for your application. The load range and maximum weight capacity are indicated on the tire sidewall. A tire with a higher load index than that of an OEM tire indicates an increase in load capacity. A tire with a load index equal to that of an OEM tire indicates an equivalent load capacity. A tire with a lower load index than an OEM tire indicates the tire does not equal the load capacity of the original.

Typically, the load index of tires used on passenger cars and light trucks ranges from 70 to 110. Trailer tires should be at the high end of this scale. Let's look at a very simple example: Suppose you have a Corvette on your car trailer. The trailer tires will need to support not only the weight of the Corvette but the weight of the trailer as well. That means a tire designed for a Corvette simply won't be strong enough for your trailer plus the load. See the accompanying charts for more information on load range and load index.

Check the valve stems for cracking and deterioration the same way you check your tires, and replace them any time you purchase new tires.

Triple-axle trailers are designed to carry a tremendous amount of weight. Unfortunately, toll roads charge per axle and this type of rig can get expensive. If you tow a great deal, ask yourself if a dual-axle trailer will meet your needs.

The 4406 on the right means that the tire was produced in the 44th week of 2006.

TRAILER TIRE WEAR

There are a number of important factors that influence tire wear. First, tread life is directly related to how much weight the tire has to carry. You probably subject your trailer to maximum loads all the time, and all of this weight is transferred to the tires. Overloading a tire will break down the structure of the tire and cause it to wear quickly.

Trailer tires are exposed to a far greater variety of conditions than automobile tires. Trailer tires often sit unused for an extended time period; when they are in service, the tires are used at or near maximum loads during hot weather. It doesn't get much worse for a tire. Very few people wear out trailer tires. Instead, the tires usually just rot from sitting in the sun.

How Old Are My Trailer Tires?

Exposure to sun and weather for an extended length of time will cause the rubber on a tire to crack, especially in the tire's sidewall. Part of your trailer maintenance program should be to constantly check the tires for aging. Tires that are over five years old should be inspected regularly, because cracking gets progressively worse as time goes on.

You can determine the tire age by looking at the DOT number. The DOT tire identification number is on one side of every DOT-approved tire and indicates that the tire meets all

continued on page 83

This trailer was sitting for almost a year. The inner construction of the tires has been destroyed; there's no integrity left in the tires.

STORING YOUR TRAILER AND PROPER TIRE MAINTENANCE

- Ideally, a trailer in storage should be placed on blocks to remove weight from the tires.
- If the trailer can't be put on blocks, follow these steps for tire protection.

  o Unload the trailer so that a minimum amount of weight will be placed on the tires.

  o Inflate the tires to recommended operation pressure, plus 25 percent.

  o Don't exceed the rim manufacturer's inflation capacity.

  o Make sure the storage surface is firm, clean, well-drained, and reasonably level.

  o Avoid moving the trailer during extremely cold weather.

  o Move the trailer at least every two months to prevent ozone cracking in the tire bulge area, as well as flat-spotting from prolonged strain of the sidewall and tread deflection.

  o Adjust the inflation before putting the trailer back on the road.

Cut four squares of wood to take along on trips. Should you find yourself parking on hot asphalt, you can place the squares under the tires. The wood will protect your tires as well as the parking lot.

SOME BASIC TRAILER TIRE GUIDELINES

ST Tires

- ST tires feature unique materials and construction to meet the higher load requirements and demands of trailer applications.
- The polyester cords in an ST tire are larger than those in a comparable passenger-car or light-truck tire.
- The steel cords have a larger diameter and greater tensile strength to meet additional load requirements.
- The rubber compounds used in an ST tire contain more chemicals to help the tires resist weather and cracking from ozone exposure.

Inflation

- Always inflate trailer tires to the maximum inflation recommended by the manufacturer that built your trailer.
- Check inflation when the tires are cool and haven't been exposed to the sun.
- If the tires are hot to the touch after highway driving, add 3 psi to the normal maximum inflation.
- Underinflation is a common cause of trailer tire failure.

Load-Carrying Capacity

- All of your trailer tires must be identical in size for the tires to properly manage the weight of the trailer.
- The combined load capacity of the right and left tires should always equal (or exceed) the gross vehicle weight capacity of the axle.
- The combined capacity of all of the tires should exceed the loaded trailer weight by at least 20 percent.
- If the actual loaded weight is not available, use the trailer GVW. Even better, load your trailer with a normal load and have it weighed. The results might surprise you.
- If a tire fails on a tandem-axle trailer, replace both tires on that side. The remaining tire was probably subjected to excessive loading and could have been damaged internally.
- If you replace the tires on your trailer with tires of a larger diameter, the tongue height may need to be adjusted in order to maintain proper weight distribution.

Speed

- As heat builds up, a tire's structure starts to disintegrate and weaken. A tire that's been going flat without your noticing it will have this problem.
- The load-carrying capacity of a tire gradually decreases as the heat and stress generated by higher speed increase.

Time

- Time and exposure to the elements weaken a trailer tire much more than use.
- After three years, roughly one-third of a tire's strength is gone.
- Trailer tires should be replaced after four to five years of service regardless of tread depth or tire appearance.
- If you store your trailer outside, shield the tires so the sun won't dry out the sidewalls.

Storage

- The best place to store a trailer is in a cool, dark garage with the tires at maximum inflation.
- Place thin plywood sheets between your trailer tires and a concrete floor.
- Put your trailer on blocks to take the weight off the tires.
- Lower the air pressure and cover the tires to protect them from direct sunlight if you leave the trailer outside.

Maintenance

- Clean the tires using mild soap and water.
- Do not use tire-care products containing alcohol or petroleum distillates.
- Inspect tires often for any cuts, snags, bulges, or punctures.
- Check the inflation of the tires before towing and again before the return trip.

Mileage

- Trailer tires seldom wear out. They're made of a rubber compound much harder than that of the average passenger-car tire.
- The life of a trailer tire is generally limited by time and duty cycles. You'll get very little tread wear on the average trailer.

WHEELS AND WEIGHT RATINGS

- Make sure wheel ratings are compatible with tire ratings. For example, don't mount a tire rated at 3,000 pounds on a wheel rated at 2,000 pounds.
- If ratings aren't marked on the wheel, check with the trailer manufacturer and wheel manufacturer for proper information.
- Don't automatically assume the tires on a used trailer are suitable for the wheels.
- When buying radial tires to replace bias-ply tires, be sure to match tires and wheels to avoid serious problems. Remember, all the wheels and tires on your trailer should be the same size and from the same manufacturer.

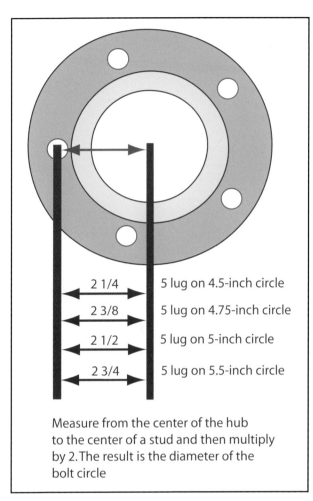

2 1/4	5 lug on 4.5-inch circle
2 3/8	5 lug on 4.75-inch circle
2 1/2	5 lug on 5-inch circle
2 3/4	5 lug on 5.5-inch circle

Measure from the center of the hub to the center of a stud and then multiply by 2. The result is the diameter of the bolt circle

This lug-centric wheel was not installed properly. The lug nuts should be used to center the wheel and tire assembly on the axle. The small directional arrow indicates that this wheel is meant to be installed on only one side of your trailer.

continued from page 80

federal standards. It begins with the letters "DOT." The next two numbers or letters indicate the plant code where the tire was manufactured, and the last four numbers represent the week and year the tire was built. For example, the number 3106 means the tire was produced during the 31st week of 2006. A different dating system was used prior to 2000. If your trailer tires were constructed before the year 2000 (in other words, they do not use the DOT tire identification number described above), it's time to buy new tires.

Tire Covers

The simplest way to extend tire life is to cover the tires when the trailer is not in use. Ultimately, the sun will do more

One way to determine the diameter of the bolt circle is to measure from the center of the hub to a bolt. Then multiply that number by 2. This measurement is easiest if you remove the dust cover from the hub. That way you have an exact center.

damage to your tires than all of the miles you accumulate. There are a variety of ways to cover your trailer's tires; ask a tire store or trailer dealership for a recommendation.

How Important Is a Spare Tire?

If the trailer is rarely used, or is stored in the sun where dry rot can be an issue, it might be really important to have a spare. On the other hand, if you carefully inspect the trailer before each use, keep the tires in good shape, and have a dependable roadside assistance program, a spare tire probably isn't necessary.

If possible (and it usually isn't), have the wheels and tires of the trailer match those of the tow vehicle. That way, if there's a flat, one spare tire will accomplish the task no matter which wheel it is. I'm not suggesting that you drive a long distance with a passenger-car tire carrying your trailer, but it will at least get you to the next exit ramp, where you can replace the blown-out trailer tire with a real ST trailer tire.

WHEEL AND AXLE ISSUES

If you're building your own trailer, you absolutely must use an axle that was designed specifically for a trailer. The wheels on a proper trailer axle have just a little camber built into the axle. In other words, the wheels are not 90 degrees in relation to the ground. This camber, or leaning, greatly enhances tracking and allows the trailer to pull straighter.

Axle alignment with respect to the direction of pull is very important. The axle(s) should be perpendicular to the direction of pull. Perhaps even more important is that if you use more than one axle, these axles must be parallel to each other. If your axles are out of alignment, the trailer will generally follow a little to the side of the tow vehicle. Have your neighbor follow you as you drive down the interstate some Saturday morning to ensure your axles are properly aligned.

Misaligned axles can also contribute to tire wear. If you see a lot of wear on one edge of a tire, then you probably have an axle-alignment problem.

TIRE CARE DURING STORAGE

When you park your trailer for an extended period of time, make sure the trailer is as level as possible, especially if you have an enclosed trailer, as these are fairly heavy. Level storage is even more critical if you leave a car, golf cart, or other equipment in the trailer all winter.

Leveling the trailer helps prevent tire overload, which can occur due to weight transfer. You can use blocks to support the wheel positions. Take extreme care when blocking tires so that they're fully supported across the entire contact patch. Use curved tire blocks, not a leftover hunk of wood with sharp edges.

Consider using jack stands under the trailer so that the tires bear no load during storage. If the trailer is left outside, cover the tires to protect them from direct sunlight and ozone aging. Keep in mind that air loss will occur over time; check and refill your tires to the correct pressure before you use the trailer for a trip.

If you actually remove your trailer tires during the off season, store them in a clean, cool, dry, and well-ventilated area. Cover the tires with an opaque, waterproof material, such as a plastic tarp. Don't stack the tires so high that the bottom tire loses its shape. At the beginning of the next season, when remounting the tires, position them on the hub and tighten the lug nuts according to manufacturer's torque specifications.

CHAPTER 7
BRAKE SYSTEMS

I put trailer brakes in the same category as lighting: When they're working, they're wonderful; at the first sign of a problem, I have an anxiety attack.

If your trailer has brakes, you need to determine whether or not they work. If you bought a brand-new trailer, they should work just fine. If you purchased a used trailer, like I usually do, brakes can be a real crapshoot.

The laws concerning trailer brakes are different from state to state and may vary depending on the type of trailer. Some states require brakes on all trailers over a given loaded weight, while other states use the type of trailer and number of axles as a guideline. In some cases, a trailer with three or more axles must have brakes on at least two of those axles. Generally, any trailer that has a gross vehicle weight rating (GVWR) of over 3,000 pounds will need brakes. In some states, however, this requirement may be as low as 1,000 pounds. Make sure

you know and adhere to your state's laws. Your local trailer store will know the requirements for your state.

To complicate things a little, all tow vehicle manufacturers have their own guidelines for trailer weights and brakes. In a lot of cases, the weight of your loaded trailer will be greater than the vehicle you're using to tow the trailer. In this situation, there is simply no way your tow vehicle's brakes can stop the weight of the total rig. Having brakes on the trailer will give you more stability under stopping and greatly reduces the possibility of jackknifing in a panic stop.

The various brake systems described in this chapter are not as complicated as they may seem. There are two types of brakes—drum brakes and disc brakes—and they're almost exactly like the brakes on your car or truck. In addition, there are two ways to apply these brakes—an electrical system or a surge, or mechanical, system.

At least once a year, crawl under your trailer and check the brake hoses for swelling and cracks in the outer liner. Also check to see that the hoses aren't twisted.

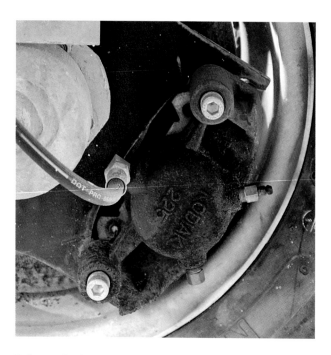

Before you begin to bleed your trailer brakes, go around to all of the bleed screws and make sure they can be loosened. If a bleeder is rusted into place or if you break the screw off, you will have to buy a new caliper.

ACTUATING THE BRAKES

Let's start with the actuation system. Trailer brakes can be operated by air, hydraulic fluid, or electrical systems. Most big commercial vehicles rely on air and hydraulic systems in which the tow vehicle and trailer use the same circuit. Almost all recreational trailers use either hydraulic surge brakes or electric brakes. Also, the trailer brakes and the tow vehicle brakes are physically separate and failure on one will not cause a complete failure on the other.

Regardless of which system is on your trailer, the end result is a pressurized application of one material (the pad or

Brake fluid lines are often very long. The fluid has to move from the tongue of the trailer to the rearmost axle; thus, the lines need to be secured in such a way that they don't run over any part of the trailer.

Brake calipers for trailers usually have two bleeder screws; one caliper can be used on both sides of the car. Remember that you should bleed the system using the uppermost bleeder screw.

shoes) against another surface (the drum or disc) to convert mechanical energy into heat energy. Brakes work with friction and demonstrate basic energy conversion. The brake pad or shoe rubs against metal, which can be a brake drum or a brake disc. When the brake material rubs against the metal, heat is created. This heat then dissipates into the atmosphere. Think back to high-school physics for a moment: You cannot destroy energy, you can only convert it.

A bigger rig will generate more mechanical energy that will need to be converted to heat energy to slow the rig down. That's why big trailers have four discs or drums. Fortunately, engineers have figured all of this out for you; you only have to know how to take care of the brakes on your trailer.

In your car or truck, you actuate the brakes, creating friction, by pushing down on the brake pedal. You don't have a separate brake pedal for your trailer, so there needs to be another way to actuate the brakes. You need a system that will apply the trailer brakes at the same time you actuate the tow vehicle brakes. There are two such systems available: a surge brake controller or an electric brake controller.

The Surge Brake Controller

Hydraulic surge brakes work as a totally self-contained braking system with no connection to the tow vehicle. This system doesn't require any electrical or hydraulic connection to the tow vehicle for the trailer brakes to work.

In this system, a surge coupler is mounted on the tongue of the trailer. Inside this coupler is a linkage that connects to a hydraulic master cylinder. When the tow vehicle starts to

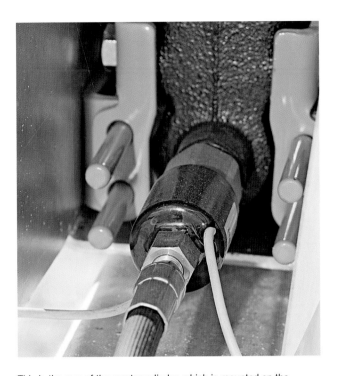

This is the rear of the master cylinder, which is mounted on the tongue of the trailer. Trailer brakes only use a single line for all of the brakes. If you have a hydraulic leak in any part of the system, you lose all the brakes. Your truck or car uses a split system.

brake, or slow down, the forward momentum of the trailer pushes on the surge coupler, causing the coupler to slide back and apply pressure against the master cylinder piston rod. The surge coupler is essentially the brake pedal for your trailer.

The mechanical force of the coupler is proportional to the difference in pressure between the two vehicles and determines the hydraulic output of the brake system. In other words, if you try to stop quickly, the coupler will put more pressure on the trailer's master cylinder than if you stopped gradually. Thus, the amount of pressure applied to the trailer's brakes will be proportional to the force exerted by the trailer's tongue against the hitch on the tow vehicle. The greater the rate of deceleration, the greater the hydraulic pressure that's applied to the trailer's brakes. After you've completed your stop and you start to move again, the forward pull on the surge coupler relieves the pressure on the master cylinder and releases the trailer's brakes.

Although surge brakes are simple, they have a couple of drawbacks. A surge braking system simply can't tell the difference between normal braking and backing up in your driveway. Since surge brakes engage when the trailer pushes on the tow vehicle, they also engage when backing up. If you're really smooth, you'll be able to back up without engaging the trailer brakes. In reality, most of us aren't that smooth, which means we need a way to temporarily disable the surge system.

The coupler is bolted in place with a surge brake system.

This is a hydraulic surge braking system. Always check the level and the condition of the brake fluid before you head out on a trip. The fluid should be clear. You can buy test strips to check the moisture content of the brake fluid.

Check the hose on the hydraulic surge system to make sure it's free of cracks and not swollen.

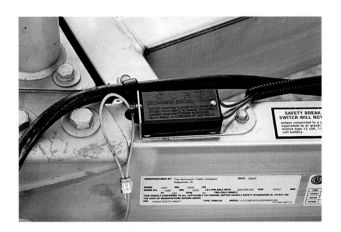

The electrical activation switch is very simple. Check periodically to ensure that it is operational.

A little electricity is the answer. When you put the transmission of the tow vehicle into reverse, the backup lights come on. The electricity from the backup lights can be routed to an electrical solenoid that will defeat the braking action of the surge coupler when you're backing up. In other words, when your backup lights go on, the trailer's braking system won't work.

Boat owners have a slightly different problem. Let's say you're backing a large trailer and boat down a steep launching ramp. The angle of the ramp will add significant pull into the water, which means you might need to use the brakes. Extra braking power from the trailer's brakes would be nice, but unfortunately, the brakes have been disabled by the reverse solenoid. In this situation, you have to back down the ramp very carefully and enter the water slowly. Surge brakes are widely used on boat trailers because electrical brakes simply don't hold up well when exposed to water. Surge brakes are also used on most rental trailers because they eliminate the need for any electrical hookups other than trailer lights.

If you're pulling a trailer in the mountains and you drive down some long descents, treat your surge brakes like truck brakes. Use regular short applications of moderate braking with intervals for cooling the brakes.

Surge brake systems historically have used drum brakes, but disc brakes are becoming popular because they dissipate heat nicely and shed water quickly. With disc brakes, the brake rotor is exposed to cool air as you go down the road. With drum brakes, a lot of the heat energy is captured and trapped within the brake drum.

In addition, disc brakes require no adjustment for pad wear. A disc brake system is designed to hold the brake pad in very close proximity to the brake rotors. Thus, when you step on the brake pedal, the pad makes almost instantaneous contact. Surge brakes are normally set up properly right from delivery and require little to no adjustment over time, especially if you have disc brakes. Drum brakes will require adjustment to the shoes for wear.

If you park your trailer for long periods of time, you may need to bleed the hydraulic system. Also, you have to lubricate the surge brake coupler so it slides easily under load. When surge brakes become troublesome, the culprit is often low brake fluid or a bent or pinched brake line.

Although surge-actuated brakes suffer from some idiosyncrasies, they're the most common braking system used on trailers. Surge brakes have been around for a long time, and their construction and installation have been refined by many years of experience. They provide a well-engineered solution to the problem of trailer braking.

The Electric Brake Controller

Electric brake actuators are an alternative to surge brake actuators. In an electric brake system, a simple sensor (usually a rheostat) is placed on the brake pedal of the tow vehicle and provides a signal when you use the brakes. The electrical signal is then amplified and used to apply braking action to the trailer. With this approach, the brakes work only when you want them, rather than engaging unnecessarily when you're backing up or driving downhill. Electric brakes can also be adjusted to balance the braking action so that the trailer brakes come on harder than the tow vehicle brakes.

Electric brake actuators require a connection to control the operation of the trailer brakes. This electric brake controller supplies the power from the tow vehicle to the trailer's electric brakes. In other words, we have wires. There are two types of electric brake controllers: proportional and time delayed.

A proportional electric brake controller senses how quickly the tow vehicle is stopping and applies the same amount of braking power to the trailer. With a proportional brake controller, once you step on the brake pedal, a motion-sensing device senses how quickly the tow vehicle is stopping. It then applies power to the trailer brakes just as quickly (or slowly) as the towing vehicle is stopping. This proportionate action allows the trailer to stop at the same rate as the tow vehicle. In an extreme stopping situation, where the driver slams on the tow vehicle's brakes, a proportional controller will immediately send maximum power to the trailer brakes. This type of brake controller provides the smoothest and quickest braking while also providing the least amount of wear on both the vehicle and trailer's brakes.

With a time-delayed trailer electric brake controller, once you step on the brake pedal, the predetermined amount of power (set by the user and based on trailer weight) is sent back to the trailer brakes. With time-delayed controllers, a delay always exists from the time the brake pedal is pushed to the time the unit reaches the user-set, maximum braking output. The delay can be shortened or lengthened with a switch. If the switch is set too low, the tow vehicle will do most of the initial braking, putting extra strain on the vehicle's brakes. If the switch is set too high, the trailer will brake harder. In most cases, either the truck or the trailer will do the majority

This electric drum brake is one of the cheapest brake systems available, which accounts for its popularity. It's very common on RV trailers and is generally trouble free.

The cable you see in front of the black battery box attaches to the tow vehicle as part of the breakaway brake activation system. If the tow vehicle and the trailer become separated, the cable will pull on the switch in the small black box, activating the trailer brakes. The battery must be fully charged for this system to operate.

of the braking, resulting in uneven brake wear. The trick is for you to get the switch set to the correct setting.

Even though the two controllers' methods are different, they have some similarities. Both systems allow the driver to adjust the maximum braking power to match the weight of the load being towed. Both have a manual override trigger that can be used to apply only the trailer brakes, and both have the same wiring configuration for installation.

The differences between proportional and time-delayed brake controllers include cost, braking performance, wear and tear, calibration, size, use, and safety. Time-delayed controllers are normally cheaper, although this cost difference has decreased in recent years. Time-delayed controllers always send the same braking power to the trailer, while proportional controllers will vary the braking power based on how quickly the tow vehicle is stopping. Thus, the proportional controller produces smoother braking action. Time-delayed systems will cause more wear on either the trailer or vehicle brakes, because one or the other will do the majority of the braking. Proportional controllers, on the other hand, reduce wear by spreading the braking power evenly.

Time-delayed controllers typically don't require calibration, while some proportional brake controllers do need calibration to work properly. Most newer proportional models are self-calibrating or are simple to calibrate. Time-delayed controllers are traditionally smaller and slimmer than proportional controllers, but newer proportional controllers are more comparable in size and shape. Time-delayed controllers are best for casual users. A proportional controller is ideal for a trailer that will be towed frequently, because it operates

well in a variety of towing conditions and causes less wear on the braking systems. Proportional brake controllers provide additional safety because they automatically ramp up to full power if the tow vehicle makes an emergency stop. It's all about choices.

ELECTRIC BRAKES

Electric trailer brakes are similar to the hydraulic drum brakes used on your car or truck. They differ only in the way they're actuated. Car and truck brakes are actuated by hydraulic pressure, generated by the master cylinder, which expands the wheel cylinder. When the wheel cylinder expands, the brake shoes are forced into contact with the brake drum.

Electric brakes function by the action of an electromagnet inside the brake drum. When the brake controller sends voltage to the electromagnet, it is attracted to the rotating armature surface of the drum. The friction of the magnet against the armature surface actuates a lever that expands the brake shoe out against the drum surface—the same thing that occurs within a hydraulic brake when the wheel cylinder expands. When you take your foot off the brake pedal and the vehicle starts to move again, current to the magnet is cut off and the brakes are released. Varying the amount of voltage supplied to the magnets will vary the braking effort.

Routine maintenance of electric trailer brakes is less involved than hydraulic surge brakes, but the electric units require more investment in wiring and time. The simplest part of any electrical system for any trailer is a good ground contact.

This battery activates the emergency breakaway braking system. Notice the small ground wire attached to the trailer tongue; the ground contact should be cleaned periodically.

This brake adjuster has one star wheel, generally called a uniservo. If you have two pushrods exiting the wheel cylinder, it's referred to as a duoservo wheel cylinder. Both systems work effectively, but most trailer manufacturers use the less expensive uniservo wheel cylinder.

The brake adjuster is designed to spread the brake shoes apart to keep the lining material in close proximity to the brake drum, ensuring that the response, or actual contact, takes less time. As the friction material on the brake shoe wears, you have to adjust the brake shoes to keep them in close proximity to the brake drum.

Many new trucks come with a dedicated four-pin connector under the dash specifically for electric brake controllers, while other trucks include it as part of a towing package. Unfortunately, these truck-to-trailer connectors have yet to be standardized. Given the increasing complexity of modern truck electrics and the fact that the majority have separate turn and brake-lamp circuits (while trailers use primarily a combination turn/brake), it's a good idea to let the factory build in the tow wiring from day one. Factory-installed towing packages may be one of the best bargains around.

BREAKAWAY SYSTEMS

Federal law requires that all trailers with brakes have some type of emergency breakaway system that will automatically apply the brakes if the trailer separates from the vehicle that's pulling it. On trailers with electric brakes, this means having an emergency battery backup system that can energize the brakes. This small battery, on the trailer itself, will engage the trailer brakes if the trailer disconnects from the tow vehicle.

You will also need a breakaway switch or pull pin connected to the tow vehicle to activate the brakes if the trailer comes loose. With surge brake systems, a cable or chain connected to the tow vehicle is typically used to apply the trailer's brakes in an emergency. When the chain is pulled tightly, which happens if your hitch fails, the chain pulls on the brake cylinder, applying heavy braking force and stopping the trailer.

DISC VERSUS DRUM BRAKE OPERATION

A hydraulic surge brake system is the most common trailer braking system and can be used with either drum or disc brakes. The decision between drum and disc brakes is complicated by several factors.

Earlier in this chapter, I explained that hydraulic surge brakes function by converting the inertial difference in pressure between your tow vehicle and your trailer into a mechanical pressure that's applied to the pushrod of the surge brake coupler. The difference in pressure between the two vehicles is dependant upon the rate of deceleration of the tow vehicle during braking. At a given rate of deceleration, a more heavily loaded trailer will have a greater differential pressure between itself and the tow vehicle than will a lighter trailer. Thus, the hydraulic pressure from the surge brake coupler will be higher for a heavier trailer than for a lightly loaded trailer.

Let's compare the hydraulic brake pressure output from identical brake couplers for two different trailers. The first trailer has a 22-foot boat with a gross vehicle weight (GVW) of 4,000 pounds. The second trailer has an 18-foot boat and a GVW of 2,000 pounds. If you try to stop both trailers with the same rate of deceleration, the trailer with the greater weight will have higher hydraulic brake pressure from the surge coupler. Four thousand pounds will put a lot more pressure on the surge actuation device than 2,000 pounds,

Drum brake maintenance is an important part of trailer upkeep. Drum brakes need adjustment at regular intervals, and routine inspections are vital, as parts can wear out.

This is the drum apparatus for a hydraulic brake system. The wheel cylinder is at the top, and the adjuster is at the bottom.

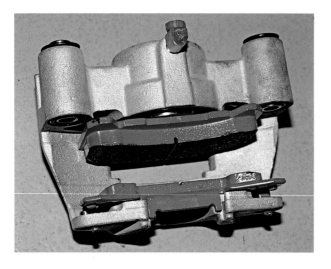

The brake pads for the outer position are often different from the pads in the inner position.

meaning a light trailer will need brakes that perform with lower hydraulic pressures.

Most hydraulic surge brake couplers will produce up to about 700 psi in panic-stop conditions. During average braking conditions, most surge brake couplers produce from 300 to 650 psi.

To complicate matters, disc brakes require higher pressures for effective braking than do drum brakes. A lighter towed load, such as the 18-foot boat in the example above, probably wouldn't have effective braking with disc brakes because it wouldn't push against the actuating lever hard enough.

In contrast, a heavier towed load, such as the 22-foot boat, would have a much better braking response with disc brakes, because the greater weight would cause greater pressure on the actuator. This pressure would create higher hydraulic output pressure, and the disc brakes would work just fine.

Most trailer drum brake systems use what's called a "uniservo wheel cylinder." That simply means they have a single pushrod. When hydraulic pressure is increased in a uniservo wheel cylinder system, this single pushrod is extended. It then pushes against the primary shoe, moving the primary shoe in an arc. The end of the secondary shoe is anchored on the brake cluster backing plate, resulting in both the primary and secondary brake shoes having levered force applied to them. Because of this levered force, drum brakes will give better braking torque at a lower hydraulic pressure. This means they're more effective for lighter loads.

In addition, the surface area of the pads on a drum brake system is normally larger than that of a comparable disc brake system. The larger the surface area of the drum brake system, the more friction you have, and it's friction that creates your stopping power. A greater area of friction means greater stopping power. Put simply, big brakes can stop better than small brakes.

Let's get back to the basic decision of drum versus disc brakes. It's best to install drum brakes on trailers that have a GVW of less than 3,000 pounds. When you get to trailers over 3,000 pounds GVW, the braking performance is relatively comparable for both drum and disc brakes.

When making this decision, you have to match the volumetric requirements of the total brake system load to the volume output capacities of the master cylinder of the brake coupler. Wheel cylinders on drum brake clusters normally require more hydraulic fluid than disc brakes.

Hydraulic drum brake units require manual adjustment to keep the brake lining in close proximity to the drum. As the lining on the brake shoes wears, the distance between the brake lining and the drum obviously becomes greater. As

BRAKE SYSTEMS

All brake rotors are designed to dissipate heat. In order to do this properly, they need to be a certain thickness. The minimum thickness is usually cast into the rotor. You cannot machine the rotor below that thickness without expecting consequences. Put new rotors on your trailer when you install new brake pads.

Just as brake rotors have a minimum thickness, so brake drums have a maximum diameter. When the diameter gets too large, the shoes can't effectively make contact. In this case, the maximum diameter is 10.09 inches

The caliper-mounting pin fits into this hole. If you're going to keep the same calipers on your trailer, clean the bushing and also use disc brake lubricant on the slider pins. It's critical that the brake calipers move on the pins.

the shoes of drum brakes wear down, the wheel cylinder and pushrod must move farther out each time you step on the brakes. This increased action requires more hydraulic fluid movement for each wheel cylinder.

As the brake lining wears down, the volume requirements of the wheel slave units will come close to, or exceed, the volumetric output capabilities of the master cylinder. When this occurs, the movement of the surge brake coupler will be extreme and will cause a notable noise as the trailer is stopped and then moved forward after braking. This noise is typically a sign that your brakes need adjustment, although it may be the sign of a bad brake coupler shock damper.

Keep in mind that the more drum brake units you have on a trailer, the more sensitive the system is to

proper brake adjustment. If you have two drum brakes, it's relatively easy to match the levels of adjustment. When you have drum brakes on two axles, you have to match the braking power of the four brakes. Properly adjusting more than two brakes is almost an art. If you have four drum brake units on your trailer, consider having a professional adjust them for you.

Disc brakes don't require adjusting. They self-adjust as the pads wear down. Because of this self-adjustment, and the very limited distance that disc brake pads move per braking application, the volumetric requirements for each disc brake wheel unit will normally be lower than the average volumetric requirements for a drum brake wheel cylinder.

HOW MUCH IS ENOUGH?

If you have a tandem- or triple-axle trailer, should you install brakes on all the axles? The quick answer is yes, because any trailer that has two or three axles and doesn't have brakes on all axles can be a problem. Generally, multi-axle trailers should have brakes on each axle. Brake systems aren't all that expensive and more than pay for themselves in increased safety and performance.

To estimate your brake system capacity, rate the brake system stopping capacity at the same value as the axle capacities. In other words, if you have a single-axle trailer with one 3,500-pound axle, calculate your stopping capacity at 3,500 pounds. If you have twin axles and both are 3,500-pound axles, then you should estimate your brake capacity to be about 7,000 pounds. Don't base your brake needs on your usual load, but rather base your calculations on the maximum load capacity of the trailer. At some point, you will likely load your trailer right to the limit and you'll need maximum braking power.

Remember that these numbers are provided as a rule of thumb and aren't to be used as design estimates for the stopping capacity of any trailer. The values discussed above are only applicable to properly adjusted, properly operating braking systems. Your local trailer store can give you a tremendous amount of guidance regarding braking needs and capacities. Get to know them and trust them.

CHAPTER 8
HITCHES AND OTHER FUN THINGS

HOW MUCH DOES YOUR TRAILER REALLY WEIGH?

Many trailer owners don't often think about the weight of their loaded trailer. Pulling too much weight can be risky business. Consult the owner's manual to find your vehicle's towing capacity, including the maximum gross trailer weight (GTW) and tongue weight (TW) the tow vehicle can handle. Tongue weight is the downward force exerted on the hitch ball by the trailer coupler. There is a limit as to how much you can put in or on your trailer. Both the tow vehicle and the hitch system have weight capacities. You must pay attention to these limits.

Gross Trailer Weight

Before you run out and spend a bunch of money on extra towing equipment, check to see exactly how much your trailer weighs when it's loaded. Then calculate how much weight you're putting on the trailer hitch. Remember that gross trailer weight is the weight of the trailer fully loaded, just the way you'll tow it down the road. This GTW is measured by placing the fully loaded trailer on a scale. The entire weight of the trailer should be supported on the scale.

Park your loaded trailer on a scale with the tongue jack post (on the front of the trailer) still on the scale platform. Block the trailer wheels, unhitch the tow vehicle, and get your total weight. This measurement is the curb weight (GTW) of the trailer. Now, move the trailer and place a jack stand (or 4x4-inch blocks) under the coupler (beyond the scale) so that the tongue jack post is supported off the scale and the trailer is fairly level. Note this weight. Subtract the little number from the big number for the hitch weight (tongue weight).

The universal rule is that 10 to 15 percent of a trailer's gross weight should be loaded in front of the leading axle. That means that 85 to 90 percent of the weight of the trailer will be carried by the running gear of the trailer. The balance between the hitch weight and the weight placed

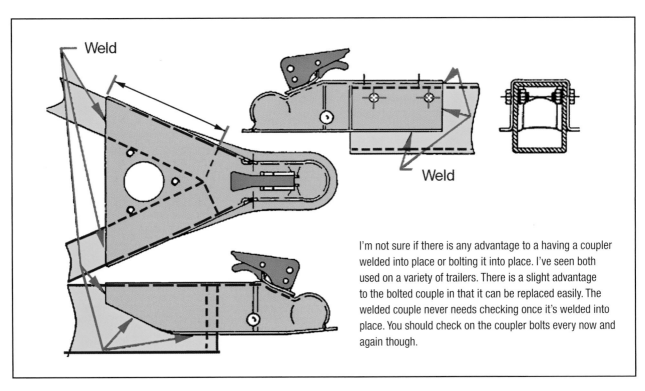

I'm not sure if there is any advantage to a having a coupler welded into place or bolting it into place. I've seen both used on a variety of trailers. There is a slight advantage to the bolted couple in that it can be replaced easily. The welded couple never needs checking once it's welded into place. You should check on the coupler bolts every now and again though.

To measure the tongue weight on my trailer, I cut a 2x4 to a height that makes my trailer parallel to the ground. I then roll the race car back and forth on the trailer to get the tongue weight correct.

Now here's a heavy-duty hitch. The lunette ring attaches to a pintle hook on the tow truck. You can easily tow a 60,000-pound trailer with this arrangement.

on the running gear of the trailer is critical for handling. Many problems with trailer sway are caused by improper tongue weight.

Another Way to Measure Tongue Weight

Tongue weights of up to 300 pounds (which means you have a trailer that weighs around 3,000 pounds) can easily be measured on a household scale by simply resting the trailer coupler on the scale and placing the scale on a box so that the coupler is at its normal towing height. For an accurate measurement, the trailer must be fully loaded and level.

For tongue weights above 300 pounds, place a household scale and a brick that's the same thickness as the scale 3 feet apart. Set a length of pipe on each, and then rest a beam across these pipes. Now, zero the scale to correct for the weight of the beam and pipe. Make sure that you block the trailer wheels during this exercise. Rest the trailer jack on the beam, 1 foot from the brick and 2 feet from the scale.

To obtain the tongue weight, multiply the scale reading by three. Remember that the average household scale only reads to about 300 pounds. Some of the digital scales may go higher, but I would be careful here. If your tongue weight is going to be over 300 pounds you may need to move the scale and brick to 4 feet apart. Be careful with your calculations.

Don't forget to take into account the weight you're carrying in the truck bed, cargo area, or trunk of your tow vehicle. Five hundred pounds of tools in the bed of your truck has the same effect on the rear springs of your truck as 500 pounds of tongue weight. That means you've effectively reduced the load capacity of your trailer.

Balancing the Weight

You can do a lot to improve weight balance by paying attention to how you load your trailer. If you get the weight distribution wrong, your trailer will sway back and forth across the road.

Let's say, for example, you go to a home improvement store and buy a bunch of concrete blocks and some framing studs. You bring your small utility trailer that's designed to hold up to 2,000 pounds. Because the concrete blocks are heavier than the framing studs, you should first spread the blocks out evenly over the entire floor of the trailer and then place the studs evenly on top of the blocks. Don't stack all of the concrete blocks on one side of the trailer and the framing studs on the other side, because this will cause one side of the trailer to be much heavier than the other side.

Remember that axle capacity is the load to be carried by the axle(s). If the weight is shifted off-center or to one side of the trailer, the load placed on that side might be too great for the axle. You can overload the trailer axle, even though your total trailer weight may be fine. The load on the heavier side should never exceed one-half the rated capacity of the axle(s). Even though you might have an axle that's rated at 2,000 pounds, you cannot load all of the weight on just one side of the trailer. The 2,000-pound rating pertains to a load that is centered.

If your hitch weight is less than 10 percent of the gross trailer weight, you can correct for this by loading heavy supplies, such as tools, as far forward as possible. If your recreational trailer's water tank is behind the axle(s), travel with as little water in the tank as possible to reduce weight in the rear. Trailers with water tanks located in front usually handle

This heavy-duty hitch has equalizer bars and a huge range of adjustability. It may be overkill for most people, but this setup ensures your trailer will tow level.

best when the tanks are full, because the water adds to hitch weight. I hope you're getting the idea here.

HITCHES

After you've determined how much weight you'll be towing and how much weight your tow vehicle can handle, you can select a hitch. Trailer owners generally spend too little time considering the various choices for a hitch. Yet the hitch is perhaps the most important factor in ensuring that your tow vehicle and load make it to their destination safely.

There are several types of hitches to choose from. In most cases, the trailer you're towing will determine the type of hitch you'll need. The hitch must not only be strong enough to hold the gross weight of your trailer, it must also fit on your tow vehicle.

Hitch Classes

Class 1 hitches are light-duty trailer hitches suitable for most vehicles, including small and compact cars. Towing capacity for this hitch class is up to 2,000 pounds. Maximum tongue weight is 200 pounds. Class 1 hitches should be limited to use with smaller trailers, such as a utility trailer less than 6 feet in length or a boat trailer no longer than 14 feet. These hitches are available either with a permanent draw bar (or tongue) or a sport frame style, which has a removable draw bar that inserts into a permanently mounted receiver. Some models attach directly to the bumper; others attach to both the bumper and the frame.

Since most modern cars don't have traditional bumpers, you'll only find this basic bumper hitch on light trucks. A bumper hitch should only be used with very small trailers.

Most motorhomes are equipped with receiver hitch arrangements for towing. The electrical connections are essentially the basic system. Motorhome receivers normally have a 2x2-inch opening and are suitable for a 5,000-pound towing weight.

Always install the receiver pin and clip. The most common size is 1/2 inch; larger receivers are often 5/8 inch.

Notice that sufficient thread is visible below the hitch ball nut.

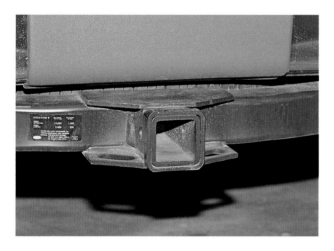

The extra bracing above and below the receiver adds a tremendous amount of strength.

Class 2 hitches are medium- to heavy-duty hitches suitable for midsize and larger vehicles, including minivans. A Class 2 hitch isn't recommended for use with compact cars. Compact car suspensions simply aren't adequate for this type of hitch. Class 2 hitches can safely pull a utility trailer up to 12 feet long or a boat trailer up to 20 feet long. They attach to the vehicle frame and usually incorporate a receiver and a removable draw bar. Towing capacity for this class is up to 3,500 pounds. Maximum tongue weight is 300 to 350 pounds.

Always secure the pin that holds the ball mount in the receiver. In this case, it's not only secured from sliding out, but also from theft.

Class 3 hitches are heavy-duty hitches suitable for trucks, vans, and SUVs. They use heavier mounting hardware and an undercar receiver that attaches directly to the vehicle's frame. Hitches in this class can easily pull a car or boat trailer up to 24 feet long. The towing capacity ranges from 3,500 to 7,500 pounds, depending on the style of hitch. Tongue weight ranges between 300 and 500 pounds. The towing capacity and tongue weight can be increased beyond these limits if the hitch incorporates a weight-distribution system—a mounting arrangement that distributes weight directly to the frame and transfers the weight to all four wheels of the tow vehicle. A weight-distribution system, or equalizer system, is safer and better for heavy-duty towing because it improves handling in the tow vehicle and allows the vehicle to tow heavier loads without sagging in the rear.

Class 4 hitches can tow up to 10,000 pounds, and Class 5 up to 14,000 pounds. Both use a weight-distribution, or equalizer, system to transfer this weight to all four of the vehicle's wheels. Class 5 hitches utilize the heaviest hardware and are generally a welded single body. These hitches are designed for use with full-size trucks and vans. You'll also find them used with three-quarter-ton and one-ton trucks for commercial towing. They're designed to handle very large loads, such as large horse trailers, enclosed car trailers, boat trailers more than 24 feet long, and large campers.

You may have to turn the hitch mount around to get the trailer to tow properly.

This conventional pin box hitch has an extension. By extending the pin out, the system can be used on a short-bed truck. (Anything less than 8 feet is considered short.) This extension creates greater space between the trailer and the truck cab. You normally have 52 inches between your trailer nose and the truck cab.

Hitch Types

Trailer hitches come in a variety of shapes and sizes for various applications. Generally speaking, trailer hitches are classified as weight-carrying or weight-distributing. The best type for you depends entirely upon the tow vehicle, trailer size, and trailer weight.

- Weight-carrying hitches are used in applications where trailer weight is less than 3,500 pounds, and where the weight and suspension of the tow vehicle can accommodate that load. The tongue weight is carried directly on the rear of the tow vehicle and on the hitch.
- Weight-distributing hitches redistribute the hitch tongue weight and are normally used for heavier trailers up to 10,000

HITCH CLASSES

Class 1
Hitch type: light duty
Gross trailer weight: up to 2,000 pounds
Tongue weight: 200 pounds

Class 2
Hitch type: medium to heavy duty
Gross trailer weight: up to 3,500 pounds
Tongue weight: 300 pounds

Class 3
Hitch type: heavy duty, undercar receiver
Gross trailer weight: up to 5,000 pounds
Tongue weight: 300–350 pounds

Class 4
Hitch type: undercar receiver
Gross trailer weight: up to 10,000 pounds
Tongue weight: up to 1,000 pounds

Class 5
Hitch type: undercar receiver
Gross trailer weight: up to 10,000 pounds
Tongue weight: up to 1,200 pounds

pounds. These weight-distributing hitch attachments are sold separately and slide into a Class 3, 4, or 5 weight-carrying receiver hitch. They typically use two spring bars, one on each side of the trailer, to lift up and apply leverage to the tow vehicle. This redistributes the tongue weight from the rear axle to the front axle of the tow vehicle. This distribution provides greater vehicle stability while towing. Weight-distributing hitches currently come in two configurations: one with square bars, called trunnion bars, which hook to the center of the ball mount, and one with round bars that slide into the bottom of the ball mount.

Hitch Height

I've said this before, but I can't stress it enough: Your trailer should always ride level to the ground. There really isn't an excuse for not following this rule. The hitch companies make a lot of different units that allow you to level your loaded trailer. You can easily purchase a ball mount that is lower or higher than the receiver.

If you have a small utility trailer, you can use a drop hitch to level things out. The most common is the 2-inch drop. Your local auto parts store should have a nice selection of drop hitches. If you need more than a 3- or 4-inch drop, you might have to get it from a trailer store.

Trailer stores also carry adjustable drop hitches. If you own several trailers, then an adjustable drop hitch might be

A glider, or slider, hitch allows the hitch plate to glide back almost a foot, allowing more cab clearance in tight turning maneuvers.

This hitch has a large range of adjustment. I prefer pins (as opposed to bolts) for attachment; they allow you to make adjustments much more easily. I also like the idea of having four different hitch balls. Note that the chains are not hooked up properly; they should cross under the hitch.

best for your situation. Regardless of how you choose to do it, be sure to level out the trailer.

Getting the Correct Hitch Ball

There are several things to consider when selecting a hitch ball. First, make sure the hitch ball weight rating is greater than the gross trailer weight. Next, the hole diameter on the ball mount shouldn't be more than 1/16 inch greater than the ball shank diameter. In other words, the hitch ball and the ball mount should be a close fit.

Finally, when you tighten the ball down, always use the lock washer and make sure a portion of the ball shank extends past the bottom of the nut. There are four pieces of information you need to get the correct hitch ball: GTW, hole diameter of the ball mount, ball mount platform thickness, and trailer coupler size.

HITCHES FOR FIFTH-WHEEL TRAILERS

The biggest disadvantage of the fifth-wheel compared to conventional trailers is that the fifth wheel takes up a lot of truck bed space. The fifth-wheel hitch occupies the center of the truck bed, and the hitch pin is located in front of the centerline of the tow vehicle's rear axle. Hitch weight of fifth-wheel trailers is usually around 20 percent of the trailer weight. Hitches are rated for up to 15,000 pounds of GTW. Here are some basic terms used to describe typical fifth-wheel hitch components:

- **Fifth-wheel plate:** The unit that contains the hitch plate, plate jaws, and handle. All of this is mounted in the truck bed.
- **Handle:** Used to release or lock the plate jaws.
- **Hitch plate:** The wheel that allows the trailer to rotate.

Select a hitch ball size that matches the size of the trailer coupler. Then match the size of the hole in the hitch mount to the shank diameter of the hitch ball.

Older trailers use this mechanism to lock the coupler to the ball. Today, the simple latch mechanism is much more common.

- **Pin:** The connecting device attached to a fifth-wheel trailer (designed to fit into the plate jaws mounted in the truck bed).
- **Pin box:** Structure attached to the bottom front section of the trailer frame (the pin is attached to the bottom).
- **Plate jaws:** Hold the pin.
- **Side rails:** Support rails bolted to the tow truck bed (supports the fifth wheel hitch).

If you plan to do any serious towing and handling of extremely heavy loads, you may want to consider using a fifth-wheel trailer or a gooseneck trailer. For many people, these setups offer better control. Because fifth-wheel trailers are very stable, people too often don't pay attention to balance, hitching procedures, and weight restrictions. That could be a mistake. Don't make that mistake.

GOOSENECK HITCHES

A gooseneck hitch is similar to a fifth-wheel hitch. The advantage of the gooseneck hitch is that it doesn't take up anywhere near the room in your truck bed as a fifth-wheel hitch. The gooseneck hitch is a ball mount that's mounted on a frame. Most of the time, if you need a flat bed in your truck, you can simply remove the hitch ball. Before attaching a gooseneck hitch, make sure that the truck can handle the weight you plan to haul. Don't attach a gooseneck to a pickup that has minimal power and won't be able to haul a really heavy trailer. Following are some advantages and disadvantages of gooseneck trailer hitches:

- Gooseneck trailer hitches can often handle 30,000 pounds, making them some of the strongest trailer hitches on the market today.
- They're used primarily to haul trailers that have front-end protrusions that allow you to put more stuff into the trailer.
- A lot of people need the flat surface of their truck bed when they're not hauling a trailer. There are now goosenecks available that can fold down into the bed of the truck. That way, your truck bed will be flat when you're not towing.

Having tow balls of different sizes can be very handy if you tow a variety of trailers.

- Gooseneck hitches allow you to make sharper turns than ball hitches because they're mounted in the middle of the truck bed and not at the rear of the vehicle.
- You may have to remove the truck bed to install the frame that holds the ball in place. While this may take some extra time, it's usually well worth the extra work.
- To use a gooseneck trailer hitch, you'll have to drill a hole in the middle of the truck bed.
- The ball of the hitch must rise above the actual truck bed in order to fasten anything to it.
- The gooseneck is more complicated and harder to install than a regular hitch, but it is much stronger than a regular ball hitch and can haul much more weight.

WHAT IS AN EQUALIZER HITCH?

An equalizer hitch is an attachment that allows you to transfer some of the trailer weight to the front of the tow vehicle. Load-distributing hitches—or an equalizer hitch, if you prefer—are designed to distribute the hitch weight evenly to

Notice the distance between the front of the trailer and the rear of the cab. You should have at least 52 inches to avoid contact during tight turns.

The long gooseneck hitch fits over a ball in the bed of the truck. The ball is mounted to a large frame under the bed of the truck, leaving only the ball exposed. When you're not towing, you can remove the ball to have a flat truck bed.

all axles of the tow vehicle and trailer. Evaluating the proper adjustment of a load-distributing hitch is simple. The tow vehicle should maintain the same attitude after hitching that it had before hitching. You can measure this at reference points on the front and rear bumpers.

If your truck was level before hitching, it should be level afterward, although it may be slightly lower due to the addition of the hitch weight. Level attitude means that the load is placed on the spring bars properly in order to distribute portions of the hitch weight equally to the front and rear axles. If the rear of the vehicle sags after hitching, then the spring bar loading isn't adequate.

The tow vehicle and trailer should be in a level position (attitude) in order for the hitch to do its job properly. Here is how to check:

• With the tow vehicle loaded for a trip, measure the distance between the vehicle and the ground at four reference points around the vehicle. Keep these figures handy for later use.

• Hook up the trailer and adjust the tension on the spring bars so the tow vehicle remains at roughly the same attitude. If the rear drops an inch after hitching, the front should also drop an inch.

Without an equalizing hitch, we couldn't tow trailers of any significant weight. A trailer needs hitch weight to be stable, and it's the action of distributing the weight over the entire tow vehicle that creates a bond between the trailer and vehicle. Even minor changes in the adjustment of the hitch can dramatically improve handling, so it's well worth the effort to make sure it's correct. The goal is to have the trailer riding level and the tow vehicle going straight down with the trailer connected. In this application, "straight down" means that the front of the vehicle will be pushed down from the weight of the trailer just as much as the back. You won't need to adjust the equalizer bar every time you hook up the trailer.

A pin box like this can improve the ride in both the truck and the trailer. It acts as a buffer, limiting the transfer of road impact between the tow vehicle and the trailer.

You should only have to do this when you change tow vehicles or when the load you carry changes significantly.

LEVELING YOUR TRAILER

The following list provides best practices for leveling your trailer and tow vehicle:

1. Hook up your rig with a typical load. For better balance, fill the water tank if it is in the front and empty the water tank if it is in the back.

2. Park the entire unit in a straight line on a flat, paved surface.

3. Disconnect the trailer, and move the tow vehicle forward about 6 inches.

4. If the A-frame, or tongue, is level with the mainframe rails, then you can simply measure from the bottom of the frame to the ground. Then measure from the ground to the bottom of the A-frame just behind the ball. If these measurements match, then your trailer is level. This measurement will help you determine the ball height. You can also simply place a spirit level on the A-frame and level your trailer that way.

5. Now, measure from the ground to the top of the ball on the tow vehicle. This number should be equal to or 1/2 inch higher than the trailer ball height. This setup is especially critical if the trailer has independent suspension. If the trailer has leaf springs, the ball can be 1 or 2 inches lower than the trailer, because the weight between the front and rear axles is equalized on units with leaf springs.

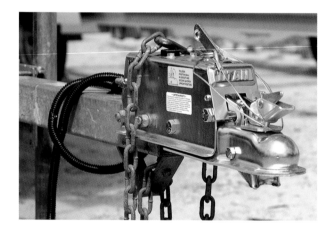

With a hydraulic brake surge actuator, no separate brake controls or connections are needed in the tow vehicle. The actuator automatically applies the trailer brakes with proportional force when the tow vehicle's brakes are applied.

6. Next, check the angle on the ball mount. The ball mount should angle back as much as possible. This angle acts like the forks of a bicycle—it keeps the unit in a straight-ahead position. To check this angle, install a bar in the ball mount and swing it parallel to the trailer frame. The end of the bar should be 4 to 5 inches off the ground when you lift it enough to remove all of the play. If the ball height is over 22 inches, then the bars can be higher off the ground.

The trailer should always ride level to the road surface. It appears that the hitch on this truck needs to be about 2 inches lower.

7. Back up the tow vehicle so that the ball is under the coupler, but don't put any weight on the ball. Put some masking tape on each corner of the vehicle, and mark the height in a convenient spot on the tape. Now we know how the vehicle sits by itself with no trailer attached.

8. Now connect the trailer and tow vehicle. Lower the trailer onto the ball, and connect the torsion bars to the link that you think might be correct (likely the first or second link). Lower the weight onto the car, or truck.

9. Now, measure the vehicle at your masking tape markings, and see how it has been pushed down. It should go down evenly on all four corners. If it is down more at the back, then you need more pressure on the torsion bars. Reconnect the torsion bar using the next link in the chain.

10. Sometimes you'll hook up the trailer and the back of your truck will be down 1 1/2 inches, while the front of your truck will be up 1/2 inch. If you pull up the next link in the chain, the back might be even, while the front is down 1 inch. You'll need something in between a normal chain link—some way to adjust a partial link. A 1/2-inch bolt pushed through two overlapping links is an adjustment of 1/3 of a link. You can use one or two bolts in the chain to create adjustments of 1/3 or 2/3 of a link.

11. If the tow vehicle doesn't go down evenly side-to-side, you can put more pressure on one bar to compensate. The right-hand torsion bar will affect the left front of the car and vice versa. Due to chassis flex, the back end of a pickup truck may twist in relation to the front when you have a poorly distributed load. In this case, it is most important to adjust the front properly. Let the back of your truck do what it wants to do and concentrate on getting the front level.

12. If you can't get the front of the vehicle pushed down, no matter how far you raise the bars up, then the torsion bars are likely too light or the receiver on the vehicle is twisting because it's too weak.

13. Once you have everything set, mark the link for future reference. I use a cable tie, but a dab of paint or nail polish works just as well. On a new hitch, the bars will work in very quickly. After a few hundred miles, you may need to use a bolt to bring the bars up 1/3 of a link.

14. Finally, install your sway control, breakaway cable, chains, and lights, and you're ready to hit the road.

Remember that during a long trip, it's always a good idea to check and, if needed, adjust the hitch as necessary when you stop for lunch or gas. Generally, you'll notice the difference right away when you head back out onto the road.

SWAY CONTROL

"Sway" is a nasty word if you're towing a large trailer. Sway means you'll feel the effects of wind gusts and sudden maneuvering. The trailer just doesn't want to go in a straight line. You can reduce sway by applying resistance to the trailer and vehicle with respect to each other. In other words, make it a little harder for your truck and trailer to react differently to wind gusts or lane changes.

There are two popular methods of sway control. The older, more common form of sway control is a friction device referred to as friction sway control. This type of unit uses friction to resist trailer sway once it has begun. Friction is used to resist pivotal movement and works against the effects of induced sway. This type of sway control device operates on the principle of stiffening the coupling between the tow vehicle and trailer. The degree of stiffening or friction can be adjusted

Notice how level and parallel to the ground this entire rig is. If you work with equalizer bars and carefully balance the weight of your load, your tow rig can be this way too.

to suit various trailer weights and towing conditions. This type of simple unit doesn't prevent the generation of sway; it simply works to resist the forces once they've started.

The newer approach uses a device controlled by dual-cam action. For example, Reese's Dual Cam Sway Control works to control sway from the start rather than just resisting sway once it has begun. In addition, this system only operates when needed. When towing in a straight line, the cams on either side of the trailer A-frame are locked in position, essentially creating a rigid connection between tow vehicle and trailer and minimizing the effects of induced sway caused by high cross-winds or passing vehicles. Normally, these cams ride in a detent, locked into position, and won't operate even on fairly sharp curves. When cornering maneuvers are required, the cams automatically slide out of their detent to permit full-radius turns. When a maneuver is abrupt, like that encountered in the event of a sudden swerve or a wheel dropping off the road, the cams seek a straight-line towing angle that helps the tow vehicle retain control.

One advantage of the dual-cam system is its ability to hold down the start of swaying activity while at the same time allowing free and easy vehicle and trailer interaction. Another advantage of the dual-cam system is that it's installed on the trailer and therefore doesn't require adjustment every time the tow vehicle and trailer are hooked up, unless hitch weight or tow vehicle loading are changed. The dual-cam system is more expensive than a traditional friction control unit.

SAFETY CHAINS

Safety chains are required for trailers regardless of the size. Safety chains prevent the trailer from separating from the tow vehicle in the event of hitch failure, such as a hitch ball that has loosened up. The chains should be crossed in an "X" fashion below the ball mount. Leave enough slack so that the

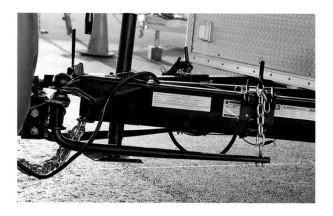

To equalize the load, adjust these bars so that the front and rear of the tow vehicle drop an equal distance. Check the final adjustment on level ground, and measure the front and rear of the tow vehicle. Once everything is level, paint the correct link on the chain with red paint to identify it easily next time.

chains don't restrict turning but at the same time keep them short enough so that the trailer coupler can't hit the ground should the hitch fail.

BREAKAWAY SWITCHES

Breakaway switches are designed to activate trailer brakes if the tow vehicle becomes separated from the trailer. Breakaway switches are required for any trailer with a gross weight of 1,500 pounds or more and manufactured after December 31, 1955. One end of the breakaway switch attaches to an electrical switch on the trailer frame, and the other end loops around a stationary hitch component on the tow vehicle. If the two vehicles become separated, this tether pulls a pin inside the breakaway switch and applies full power to the trailer brakes.

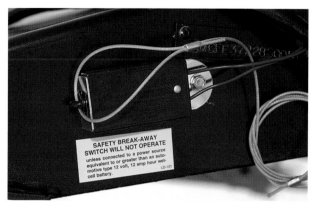

Mor/ryde's system uses a rubber spring that works in a horizontal planar motion to absorb the shock of towing and thus diminish the transfer of forces from the trailer to the truck.

Even though hitch failures are very rare, a safety breakaway switch is still recommended and may be required in your state. Be sure to adjust the cable to allow freedom to turn corners without activating the switch.

The power for this switch comes from a small auxiliary trailer battery. The switch itself should be located at or near the tongue of the trailer and consists of a boxlike device with a pin fully inserted in the switch with a long cable that attaches to the hitch of the tow vehicle. When the pin is pulled (similar to a hand grenade), the switch closes, and voltage is allowed to pass to the electric brakes on the trailer.

While hitch component failure is rare, the breakaway switch and safety chains must always be in good working order. If the pin and the cable attaching it are missing, a complete new switch should be installed on your trailer. It's so easy to do it right that there's no reason to gamble on a problem. Breakaway switches are relatively inexpensive and available at any trailer supply store.

Test this switch from time to time. To test a breakaway switch, jack up one side of the trailer, and have a partner spin the tires on that side. The tow vehicle doesn't need to be connected for this test. The trailer battery does, however, need to be fully charged. While the tires are spinning, pull the pin from the breakaway switch. The brakes should immediately lock up. If they don't, there's a problem in that circuit, and further troubleshooting is in order. If everything works properly, jack up the opposite side of the trailer to perform the same test.

Make sure your chains are heavy enough for the weight of your trailer. The positive latch pictured here is a great idea.

CHAPTER 9
TRAILER MAINTENANCE

You can remove dust caps with a big screwdriver and a mallet. Or, you can use a special pair of pliers, as seen in Chapter 12. I don't recommend reusing dust caps, especially damaged ones. New caps are quite inexpensive.

The best way to deal with the cotter pin is to use a pair of Dykes cutters to simply cut the pin out. The other alternative is to straighten the pin and tap it out with a small hammer.

Although total trailer failure is unlikely, it is possible that your lights will stop working in the middle of the night or a wheel will fall off because you forget to service the bearings. Lots of things can go wrong, but preventive maintenance stops those things from happening at inconvenient times. If you take care of your trailer components, they will work when you need them most. There are three main areas of concern: wheel bearings, brakes, and lighting. Maintenance for wheel bearings and brake systems are covered here. For lighting maintenance, see Chapter 10.

WHEEL BEARINGS

Wheel bearings are the number one cause of trailer problems, but bearing problems are mainly caused by neglect. Wheel bearing service is a task from another era. Younger people may have never heard of it, and older people have forgotten that this was once a part of traditional automotive service.

The hardest part of servicing the bearings is raising the trailer off the ground. At the very least, one side should be raised so you can remove the wheels, but it's best to get all the wheels off the ground at one time. That way, when you finish servicing the wheel bearings, you can do a quick check on the operation of the brakes. If you have a huge travel trailer, consider letting the local trailer dealer service the bearings for you.

Following are instructions for servicing your wheel bearings. Be sure to read these through at least once before starting.

Lifting the Trailer
- Park the trailer on solid, level ground.
- Block the trailer tires securely on the front and back so that no forward or rearward movement is possible.
- Loosen the lug nuts before you jack up the trailer.
- Raise the trailer following the manufacturer's instructions.
- Place the trailer on jack stands of adequate size on the front and rear.

Removing the Wheel and Hub
- Remove the wheel nuts from the wheel, and take off that wheel.
- Pry off the dust cap using a flat-bladed screwdriver and large pliers. There is also an inexpensive tool for doing this available at some auto-supply houses.

ANNUAL TRAILER MAINTENANCE

	Before Each Use	After Each Use	Quarterly	Annually	First 50 Miles	300 Miles	Before Storage	After Storage
Overall								
Wash		X					X	
Coupler								
Ensure proper fit	X							
Lubricate				X			X	X
Tongue jack								
Grease jack				X			X	
Winch assembly								
Oil gears				X			X	X
Inspect cable, rope, and straps			X					
Wheel and hubs								
Check lug nuts	X				X		X	X
Repack bearings				X			X	
Tires								
Check pressures	X						X	X
Check for sidewall cracking	X						X	X
Measure and record tread depth			X				X	X
Brakes								
Check brake fluid	X						X	X
Check brake lines	X							X
Check actuator travel			X					
Adjust brakes				X	X	X		
Check pads, rotors, or shoes and drums				X				
Electrical								
Check taillights	X							X
Check brake lights	X							X
Check trailer ground	X							

- Straighten the cotter pin that holds the bearing nut in place, and remove it. I generally use a large Dykes diagonal cutting tool. It's just a lot quicker.
- Remove the bearing nut and washer.
- Gently pull the brake drum toward you while cupping the hub opening with your hand to keep the front bearing from falling to the ground. The outer race should stay in the drum, while the inner race and bearing should come out as a unit when you remove the brake drum.
- Place the front bearing, bearing nut, and bearing washer in a clean container.

Removing the Grease Seal and Rear Bearing

- Now, place the brake drum face-down so that the back of the drum (the part that's toward the inside of the trailer) is accessible.
- Pry out the grease seal. There's a special tool for this as well, but a large pry bar works nicely. (This seal will be replaced, so you don't have to worry about damage.)
- Lift out the rear bearing, and place it in the container with the rest of the parts.
- Caution: If you are working on more than one wheel at a time, do not mix up the bearings from the different wheels.

Most bearings have numbers stamped on the inner race. Consult these numbers to find the proper replacement bearing.

You'll always damage the seal when you remove it from the hub. Don't even consider attempting to use an old seal when you perform bearing maintenance.

As shown here, there's a sequence to bearings. The larger one is usually nearest the trailer frame, with the smaller one toward the outside. Note the washer between the outer bearing and the spindle nut. The washer is a critical component.

Note the pitting on the rollers. This bearing is no longer useful and needs to be replaced.

Each bearing must stay matched with its original race. Each bearing wears differently, so they need to be kept with their respective counterparts.

Inspection

- Clean the bearings and other parts in a solvent until the grease is removed. I use brake cleaner or mineral solvents for the final cleaning.
- Place the bearing aside to dry, or blow-dry it gently with compressed air. Don't use the air pressure to spin the bearing, as you could easily damage the bearing or yourself.
- Clean the hub and spindle with mineral spirits.

- Inspect the bearing races for heat discoloration, pitting, scoring, and any unevenness.
- Inspect the bearing for damage as well. Any out-of-round rollers, cracked roller cages, or rough operation means you should replace them. Trailer bearings are typically cheap. Don't even consider reusing a bearing that has a flaw.
- Inspect the brake drum for pitting and excessive wear, especially if the brake shoes were allowed to wear down to bare metal.
- If you have electric drum brakes, inspect the brake magnet surface for excessive or uneven wear.
- If the brake drum and magnet have been saturated with grease from a failed bearing seal, replace both the shoes and magnet.

Here is the zerk fitting used on some trailers. Simply remove the dust cap to grease your bearings. Attach the gun to the small nipple in the center. NOTE: Never use an air-powered grease gun on these fittings. Use the old-style hand-powered air gun, and be careful not to blow out the inboard grease seal.

- This is a good time to have the drum turned or machined to renew the surface that comes into contact with the brake shoes.

Hand-Packing the Bearings
- Place a walnut-sized ball of wheel-bearing grease in your palm. You may want to wear latex gloves for this job.
- Take the bearing in your other hand so that the wide side is facing the grease.
- Press the bearing down into the grease in a rocking motion, and continue until the grease oozes up between the rollers.
- Force the grease into the gap between the inner races and the outer cage so that it squeezes up through the rollers and out the top.
- Rotate the bearing one-quarter turn at a time, and continue until the bearing is completely filled with grease.

Reassembly
- Put a walnut-sized amount of grease in the interior of the hub with your fingers. Spread it around the circumference of the hub.
- Place the inner packed bearing into its place in the hub.
- Put a new seal on the hub, and gently tap it into place with a hammer until it's fully seated.
- Wipe off any grease that may have gotten onto the outer surface of the seal.
- Slide the brake drum onto the axle spindle.
- Now, insert the outer bearing, a new thrust washer, and the spindle nut.

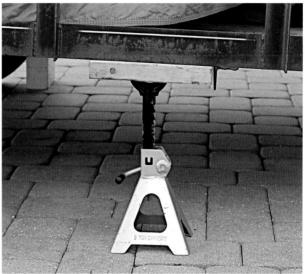

One of the key things is to make sure your trailer is properly supported when you remove the wheel to service the wheel bearings. This is a very lightweight utility trailer, so the jack stands can be small. If you have a big travel trailer, you're going to need large, heavy-duty jack stands.

Preloading the Bearings
- Tighten the axle nut by hand until it's tight. Then tighten another one-quarter turn with pliers or a wrench to set everything in place.
- Spin the drum several times to distribute the grease evenly in the bearings.
- Back off the nut with the pliers or wrench, and then retighten finger tight.
- Insert a new cotter pin to lock the nut in place, and bend it over the spindle.
- Reinstall the dust cap, wheel and tire, and hubcap. Don't forget to properly torque the wheel nuts.

New Bearings
- Bearings must always be replaced with a complete new bearing set that includes both the inner and outer races.
- The inner races are pressed into place in the hub and will have to be driven out.
- Use a brass punch to catch the edge of the race by passing it through the inverted hub. A few good whacks with a hammer should drive the old race out of the drum.
- Place the new race into position, and tap it in with the hammer and brass punch. Be very careful not to scratch the surface of the race as you pack, reassemble, and preload the bearings.

Finding Replacement Bearings and Seals
Bearings use a standardized system of numbering. If you have a factory-built trailer, contact the manufacturer to get the

continued on page 112

109

Behind the rubber cap you'll find a zerk fitting. This means the bearing has been designed to be greased simply using a grease gun. Various manufacturers have different names for this type of system. If you're rebuilding your trailer, it would be worth a trip to the trailer store to see about converting to this arrangement.

Whenever I do work on wheel bearings, I always inspect the wheel studs to make sure they are in good condition. I make sure that none of the studs have stripped threads, and that all the lug nuts take the same-size wrench.

Here's a typical bearing packing tool.

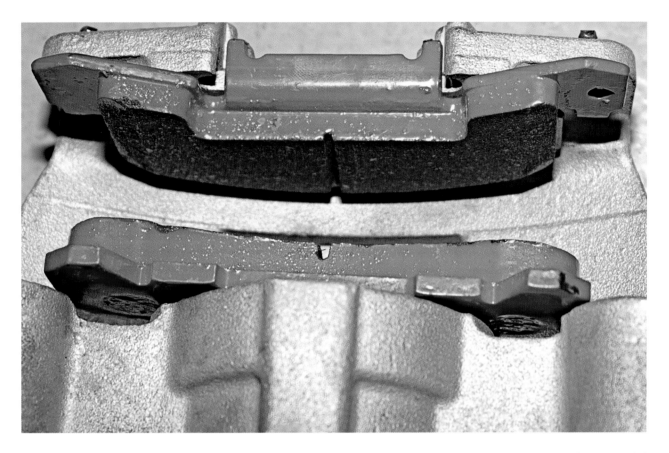

This is commonly called a loaded brake caliper. In other words, the brake caliper comes complete with the pads already in place. If you use loaded calipers in your rebuild, make sure you replace both calipers, since the friction materials have to be the same. If you have different brake pads on different wheels on the same axle, you'll get a serious pull to one side when applying the brakes.

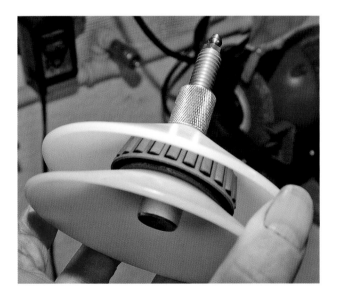

Place the bearing between the two plastic parts. Use a grease gun to shoot the grease into the bearings. The white plastic pieces will help confine more of the grease in the bearing and make less of a mess. Personally, I prefer putting on latex gloves and doing it the old-fashioned way.

Take special precautions if you are going to be working on the drum brakes from an old trailer. Many old drum brake systems contain cancer-causing asbestos.

continued from page 109

number for replacement bearings. If you don't have a clue about your trailer, you can simply remove the bearings and take them to your local bearing supply house or trailer store. They should have no trouble matching the bearings.

The same goes for seals. Seals seldom have numbers, so it's a little more difficult, but again any decent trailer supply store should be able to match them with ease. I seldom purchase bearings and seals online; it's just too tricky. Plus, the shipping usually ends up costing more than the bearings.

Bearing Buddy

The Bearing Buddy is a waterproof hub adapter found on a number of boat trailers. The Bearing Buddy takes the place of the standard dust cover and is fitted with a zerk fitting. The axle hub is filled with grease through the zerk fitting until the grease forces the Bearing Buddy piston outward about 1/8 inch. Because the piston is spring-loaded, it exerts a slight pressure (3 psi) against the grease, which maintains a slight pressure between the inside of the hub and the outside environment. When the hub is submerged, water cannot enter the hub because of this pressure.

To install the Bearing Buddy, hold it against the hub with a small block of wood, and drive it into place with a hammer. If the Bearing Buddy can't be driven into the hub or won't fit tightly, don't force it. Your hubs may be slightly oversized or undersized. If this is the case, or if the Bearing Buddy is obviously the wrong size, drive down to the trailer store.

To correctly lubricate a bearing equipped with a Bearing Buddy:

1. Remove the protective bearing cover from the hub, exposing the Bearing Buddy.
2. Attach a hand-operated grease gun (filled with bearing grease) to the grease fitting at the center of the Bearing Buddy.
3. Gently add grease.
4. When the center plate of the Bearing Buddy starts traveling forward, stop adding grease. With experience, you'll be able to feel the additional pressure against the grease gun when the Bearing Buddies are close to being filled.

Posi-lube Spindle

This bearing greasing system is very popular on boat trailers. Once again, the idea is that if you fill the entire hub area with grease, then water can't get into the bearings. With a posi-lube axle, the grease fitting leads to a tube that carries the grease to the inboard bearing and pushes the older grease back to the outboard bearing, where it comes out around the sides of the bearing. In other words, you positively lube the bearings so there's no chance of encountering an air pocket. To lubricate this bearing, perform the following steps:

- Remove the dust cap from the hub, exposing the grease fitting.
- Using bearing grease, secure the hand-operated grease gun to the posi-lube grease fitting.

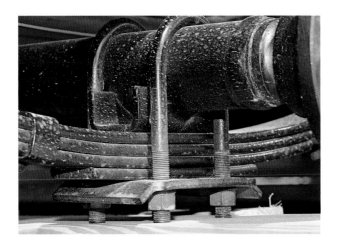

Do regular inspections of the U-bolts that hold the spring and axle together. Look for cracks and breaks.

- Gently add grease.
- When grease comes out around the outer edge of the bearing, stop pumping grease.
- Reinstall the dust cover.

Some Basic Bearing Cautions

- Never apply Bearing Buddies over posi-lube spindles. The two systems are not compatible.
- Never use an air-powered grease gun with the Bearing Buddy or posi-lube spindle covers. The force of the grease gun can damage or destroy the rear seal. If the rear seal is damaged, you'll have to replace that seal before using the trailer. Even with a hand-operated grease gun, too much pressure could damage the rear seal. Be careful.
- If you destroy the rear seal of the hub assembly and have drum brakes, grease can get onto the brake shoes and affect the performance of your brakes. In that case, you'll need to perform a complete brake job before using the trailer.
- Never reuse an old tang washer, and never use anything but an actual tang washer. Reusing the tang washer or using something other than a tang washer can cause the wheel to become separated from your trailer. These washers are so cheap you should keep a few extras in your toolbox.
- Always keep track of which bearing cone goes with which bearing cup. Don't mix them up. A cone must always remain with its matched cup.

THE BRAKE SYSTEM

If you're familiar with brakes in general, you shouldn't have many problems with trailer brakes. They aren't that different from the brakes on your tow vehicle, and they generally require the same sort of maintenance.

Boat trailer brakes are an exception. Boat trailers are special because the entire braking system gets soaked every time you launch the boat. If you use your boat in salt water, it's even worse. Salt water will corrode your brake hardware

These rollers are very easy to replace. It's hard to fathom why people keep using old, hardened, and cracked rollers on their boat trailers.

If the bearing race has to be replaced, then the bearing itself should also be replaced. The bearing and bearing race should be treated as a single unit. A failure in one means both have to be replaced.

very quickly. Plan to rebuild the brake system every three or four years if you have a boat trailer.

Quick Brake Test

The hardest part of testing the brakes is getting all the wheels off the ground. This test takes two people. One person should spin the wheel, while the other person puts a large screwdriver or pry bar in position to activate the brake coupler master cylinder. When the master cylinder is activated, the spinning wheel should come to an abrupt halt. As soon as pressure is released, the wheel should be free to spin. If your trailer fails either of these quick tests, you have a hydraulic problem. It may be best to turn this repair over to a trailer dealer.

The Annual Inspection

If you are willing to spend a half day once a year to inspect your brake system, you could save yourself some time stranded alongside the road. Set aside a Saturday to pack the wheel bearings and check the brakes all at the same time.

Inspect the condition of the drums, shoes, and shoe return springs and hardware. Replace any badly corroded

return springs and brake shoe hardware. The brake shoe adjusters should turn easily. Replace any shoes or drums that are too thin. It's a good idea to take them to a shop that works on trailers, and have them measured with a brake drum gauge. The maximum diameter for the brake drum is usually cast into the drum.

On drum brake hydraulic systems, you need to check the wheel cylinders, brake lines, and master cylinder for fluid leaks. Also, inspect the brake fluid for rust, sediment, and water contamination. You can purchase test strips that allow you to measure the percentage of water contamination or the breakdown of corrosion inhibitors in the brake fluid for a very clear indication of the fluid's condition. This test is much better than a simple visual inspection.

Brake fluid is hydroscopic, meaning it literally sucks the moisture out of the air. Thus, your brake fluid, just like your trailer tires, can go bad while your trailer is parked for long periods of time. Over time, the fluid becomes saturated with water. When the temperature of the brake fluid reaches 212 degrees, this moisture turns to steam. Because steam can be compressed, you essentially no longer have brakes on your trailer. In order for the brake fluid to reach 212 degrees, you'll have to do some heavy braking. In other words, when you need your brakes most, you won't have them.

On disc brake systems, measure the thickness of the rotors. Use a dial indicator to check for rotor runout. If the rotors are warped, worn too thin, or cracked, they need to be replaced. Check the thickness and condition of the pads, and replace them if they're worn to the minimum thickness or if the pad lining is loose or cracked. Your owner's manual might give you the specifications for these measurements. If you can't find the specs or don't know who made your trailer, then make friends with the local trailer store.

Adjusting the Brakes

As with servicing the wheel bearings, the hardest part of adjusting the brakes is getting the trailer wheels off the ground. It's not difficult with a single-axle trailer, but it gets more complicated with a twin- or triple-axle trailer. A professional trailer shop can raise the entire trailer at one time with a hydraulic lift. You, on the other hand, will have to spend some time crawling around on the ground.

With the wheels off the ground, rotate the wheel and tire while adjusting the star wheel, which allows you to change the distance the brake shoes are apart. Once the tire and wheel stop rotating, back the star wheel off 8 to 10 clicks. It's critical to get all of the brakes engaging at the same time. The secret to smooth stops is to have all of the brake shoes contacting the brake drums at the same time. This is far easier to say than it is to do. There are times I think that the drum brake adjustment process is as much art as it is science.

A slight drag on a given brake is fine. Even brake activation is more important than a slight drag on one wheel. If you have four brake drums to adjust, the process can be a little

STORING YOUR BOAT TRAILER

- Park your trailer in a protected area, such as your garage or carport. If you can't park it in a protected area, simply cover the trailer with a boat cover or tarp.
- Repack the wheel bearings to remove any lingering water or debris. If water stands on bearing surfaces for several weeks without the wheel being turned, rust will start to form, and your bearings might be damaged.
- Lubricate moving parts, such as rollers and winches, with lightweight household oil, or WD-40.

- Tighten all of the nuts and bolts on the trailer.
- Block the wheels or, better yet, raise the trailer so the tires don't come in contact with the ground.
- If your boat and trailer aren't protected in a carport, garage, or with a boat cover, you should cover the tires to protect them against ultraviolet rays.
- Block the tongue, and crank the tongue jack to the completely closed position.

REMOVING YOUR BOAT TRAILER FROM STORAGE

- Use lightweight oil to lube the winch gears.
- Check the torque of all the lug nuts.
- Check the air pressure in the tires.
- Check the tread and general appearance of the tires.
- Check the brake fluid level.

- Check the brake line for signs of deterioration or damage, and replace as necessary.
- Perform a full electrical check.
- If the trailer is equipped with Buddy Bearings or posi-lube spindles, apply additional grease.

tricky; just take your time. The process is relatively simple to explain, but it takes a while to do. You might plan on half a day the first time you try this.

Bleeding the Brakes

Most people only bleed the brakes when they replace a part in the hydraulic system. I suggest that you change the brake fluid in your trailer every two or three years as part of a preventive maintenance program.

- First, fill the brake coupler master cylinder reservoir with DOT type 3 brake fluid, available at any auto-parts store.
- Next, go to the wheel cylinder that's farthest from the master cylinder in the tubing sequence.
- Open the bleeder valve on that wheel cylinder one turn with a box end wrench or, if you have one, a brake bleeder wrench.
- Be very careful that you don't break off the bleeder valve. I soak my bleeder valves with WD-40 the day before I start the process.
- Get a piece of 5/16-inch plastic hose about 2 feet long, and push one end of the hose onto the bleeder valve.
- You'll need a clear container to catch the brake fluid. I use an old water bottle with a hole drilled in the top. Set the fluid-receiving container on top of the trailer fender or at some point above the wheel cylinder. This container should be above the wheel cylinder so that any bubbles trapped in the bleed hose will flow up and away from the wheel

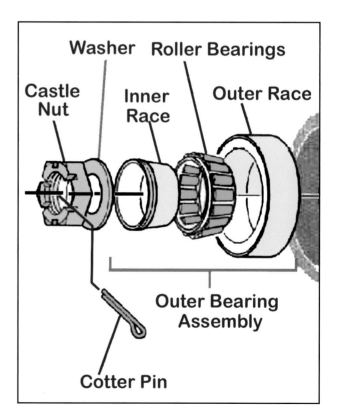

All roller bearings are similar; only the size varies. The key thing is to keep all of the components together.

cylinder, not back toward it, which would happen if the fluid container were lower than the wheel cylinder.

- Route the plastic hose from the bleeder valve to the fluid-receiving container.

- Now, go back to the brake coupler. Insert a large screwdriver into the 1/2-inch-diameter hole in the coupler. This coupler is usually under the nut on the pushrod that extends out the front of the brake coupler housing.

- With your screwdriver in this hole, use a back-and-forth motion to apply levered pressure directly to the master cylinder pushrod, bypassing the coupler and shock damper mechanism. It's nice to enlist a partner for this task.

- Remove the cap on the master cylinder reservoir and, using small 1/2-inch forward and backward strokes on the screwdriver, begin to purge air from the piston portion of the master cylinder assembly.

- Bubbles should rise from a small hole in the bottom of the reservoir. As you continue with the small back-and-forth motion, bubbles will continue to rise until the piston portion of the cylinder is full of brake fluid. Only when you see no more bubbles rising in the master cylinder reservoir should you begin making long strokes on the screwdriver to pump fluid toward the wheel cylinders.

- You need to have the piston portion of the master cylinder full of brake fluid and no more bubbles rising in the reservoir. Be careful not to look directly down into the reservoir while pumping the pushrod. The brake fluid will squirt up with considerable force during the first part of each pump stroke. Don't let it hit you in the face. You can place the filler cap on top to control this squirt, but I prefer to see the air bubbles. Just be careful.

- Now, as you pump brake fluid into the system, you'll start to see it arrive at the fluid-receiving container. Keep checking the fluid reservoir, and never let the reservoir fall below half full during this bleeding process. If the fluid gets too low and sucks air into the piston of the master cylinder, you'll have to start over. As you pump fluid through the system, the bubbles you've been seeing in the fluid-receiving container will stop. This indicates that you've completely filled the system with brake fluid, and no air is left in the system.

- Now, with the bleed hose still on the bleeder valve, close and tighten the bleeder valve. Remove the hose, and go to the wheel cylinder on the other side of the trailer to repeat the process. After bleeding the brakes, refill the master cylinder reservoir, reinstall the reservoir fill cap, and tighten.

- Next, apply pressure to the pushrod, and hold hard pressure on the screwdriver for five or ten seconds. This will develop maximum hydraulic pressure on the system and make it easy for you to see if you have any fluid leaks. After checking the system completely for leaks, you're ready to adjust the brakes.

- On electric brake systems, check the condition of the wiring, electrical connectors (especially the main trailer connector), magnets, and battery. Make sure the emergency battery is fully charged and securely mounted.

CHAPTER 10
LIGHTING AND WIRING

I recently read that for every trailer sold in the United States there are 4.3 wiring kits sold. That just goes to prove that there's one thing all trailers have in common: Sometime, in the middle of the night, and usually in the rain, your trailer lights will stop working. Although wheel bearings are the number one cause of trailer problems, electrical problems are a really close second.

If you own a trailer, you know why the average trailer owner buys over four lighting kits for every trailer he or she owns. Electrical connections and water are natural enemies. Water has been known to lie in wait for years just to get the opportunity to corrode even one crimped connector. The obvious solution then, is to keep the two antagonists—water and electricity—separated.

Electrical problems usually start with little irritants that take a few minutes to repair, such as a grounding problem or a broken wire. Eventually, your lighting system will end up with more patches than you remember making. At some point, you'll need to cut the entire wiring system out and replace it. If you don't plan ahead, this overhaul will be done late at night, just before that special trip you've been planning for years.

WIRING BASICS

Most trailers have three circuits. One is for the running lights, and one each for the left and right brake lights. Technically, you need only three wires from the tow vehicle to the trailer, plus a ground wire. The fourth wire is the ground. This means you'll need a connector with at least four contacts. Not surprisingly, the standard flat-style electrical connector for trailers uses four pins, with one enshrouded male pin on the vehicle end for the ground.

Other common connectors use five, six, or seven pins. Larger trailers sometimes use a separate circuit for running lights on the sides and front of the trailer. Other trailers use electrically actuated brakes. It's not uncommon for enclosed trailers to have interior lights or accessories powered by the vehicle battery, which requires another circuit.

As long as you concern yourself with only one circuit at a time, wiring the lights will not require reading schematic diagrams with tiny print. Just focus on one circuit at a time.

If you have a travel trailer with a separate wiring system for the interior, it operates separately from the trailer system.

These running lights come as a complete unit and can be trimmed to fit your fender.

The more expensive trailers use recessed fixtures. This light is fully protected, and yet the lens can be quickly replaced.

Simple but effective. This light is protected by a simple piece of pipe. Not only is the light fully protected—you still have easy access to the lens.

Grommet lights tend to last longer, as they allow less vibration to be transferred to the bulb filament.

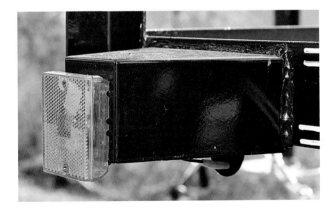

The box extends the light out from the trailer to make it more visible—but also more susceptible to damage.

This interior wiring system is similar to the wiring in your home and beyond the scope of this book.

VOLTS, AMPS, AND OHMS

In order to fully understand how the wiring in your car works, let's take a look at electricity. The three most basic units in electricity are voltage, current, and resistance. Voltage is measured in volts, current is measured in amps, and resistance is measured in ohms. Plumbing serves as a simple analogy to help understand these terms. The voltage is equivalent to the water pressure, the current is equivalent to the flow rate, and the resistance is like the pipe size.

There are two very basic rules about wire selection:

- All wire has a certain amount of resistance to current flow; the smaller the wire, the greater the resistance.
- As the amount of current (amps) increases, the resistance (ohms) increases.

Now, if we turn to the basic 12-volt electrical system in your trailer, there are two additional factors to be considered:

- Voltage drop is the primary consideration in selecting the proper electrical wire size. The length of wire in a circuit is the major contributing factor to voltage drop.
- A heavy load in an undersized wire will increase the temperature of the PVC insulation above a safe level of 180 degrees Fahrenheit. There's very little disadvantage to using a wire slightly larger than necessary and a huge disadvantage to using a wire that's too small.

Most of the budget lighting kits use 18-gauge wire. Although 18-gauge wire may be fine, there's little cost difference for 16- or even 14-gauge wire.

VOLTAGE DROP PER 100 FEET OF WIRE

The following chart explains how wire gauge causes voltage drop. Let's pretend we have 100 feet of wire. In the chart you can see what happens to the voltage for 100 feet of wire when using 18-, 16-, 14-, and 12-gauge wire. Remember, voltage drop is directly related to how long the wire is and also how thick it is. (I'm using 100 feet of wire in this example to make it easier, not because anyone has a 100-foot trailer.)

Wire Gauge	1 Amp of Current
18	1.27 voltage drop per 100 feet
16	0.80 voltage drop per 100 feet
14	0.40 voltage drop per 100 feet
12	0.32 voltage drop per 100 feet

Looking at this, we can say that the voltage drop with 18-gauge wire is 1.27 volts per hundred feet. If you use a larger diameter wire, such as 12 gauge, then the voltage drop is only 0.32 volts per hundred feet. All you really need to know is that you have less of a voltage drop with larger-diameter wire. Bigger wire is better—don't skimp on wire for any reason.

If we increase the diameter of the wire, there is much less resistance. Remember this when you wire your trailer. Most of

continued on page 119

117

Molded plastic fenders are available with the opening for the light molded right in.

U-Haul's trailer lights are well protected in this box.

Back in the day, this was the only kind of trailer light available. And you won't have any trouble finding a replacement like this today.

Here's another quick view of what happens when you use thicker wire.

Wire Gauge	Diameter (inches)	Resistance (ohms)
20	0.032	34.1
18	0.04	21.9
16	0.051	13.0
14	0.064	8.54
12	0.081	5.4
10	0.10	3.4

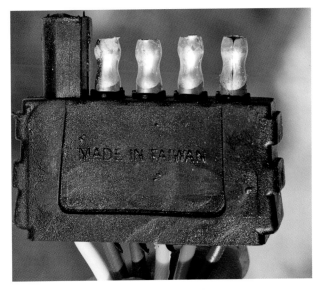

The five-way connector is the same as the four-way connector, except that the five-way has an extra red (or black) wire for auxiliary power.

Wire nuts are fast and easy to use. But you are asking for trouble when you use them on a trailer. Rest assured, they will get wet, and that will cause problems. Instead, use a butt connector and then seal the connection with some heat shrink tubing.

Water in a Hose	Electricity in a Wire	Electrical Units
Pressure	Potential (V)	Volts
Rate of flow	Current (I)	Amps
Pipe size	Resistance (R)	Ohms

continued from page 117

the flat, molded, trailer harness connectors use 16-gauge wires. It makes little sense to connect this connector to 10-gauge wires. Using 14-gauge wire on the trailer and connecting to the basic 16-gauge harness is no problem, though.

TERMINALS AND CONNECTORS

Terminals and connectors come in a variety of sizes. If you're going to do any serious trailer wiring, you might stock up on a large assortment. As with wires, it's best to buy quality terminals and connectors. When you use a crimping tool on the cheap ones, the plastic usually ends up breaking.

Blade Connectors

In this type of connection, a single blade is inserted into a blade receptacle. Both the blade and the receptacle have wires attached to them, either by soldering or crimping.

Ring Terminals

Ring terminals are also known as stud ring connectors because they can be placed over a metal stud. You'll use screws or bolts to attach them to the trailer. They offer a very positive attachment point and can't fall off unless the screw or bolt falls off. Use a little Loctite on the screw to secure it forever. The end where the wire attaches is for stranded wire.

Fork Terminals

A fork terminal is virtually the same thing as a ring connector. However, instead of a ring, the end is shaped like a fork or a "U." Be aware that if the attaching screw should loosen, the connector can drop out of place.

Butt Connectors

Butt connectors allow you to splice two wires together. There are a wide variety of butt connectors, including insulated and noninsulated. For your trailer, you may use a step-down butt connector to join two different wire gauges together.

Shrink Tubing

This vinyl tubing shrinks in diameter when it's heated. It's available in a variety of diameters and thicknesses, and its basic use is to protect the connection from dirt and water. Shrink tubing can also be used to bundle wires together and to protect them from abrasion. A heat gun works nicely to shrink the tubing, although a hair dryer works as well.

PREVENTIVE MAINTENANCE FOR LIGHTS

Always check your trailer lights before you leave home. Commercial truckers are required to make a walk-around inspection before they start each day. You should get in the same habit before you set off on an excursion with your trailer.

If the lights don't work, the most likely cause is a poor ground. Simply moving the tow vehicle backward and forward slightly may create a better ground with the trailer. Of course, this really isn't a cure as much as it is a troubleshooting technique. The next most likely cause of light failure is that dirt and oxidation have damaged the contact points of the bulb.

When you have a free Saturday morning, make sure that all of the connector-plug prongs, lightbulb sockets, wire splices, and ground connections to the trailer are clean. Then, shield them from moisture with a little petroleum jelly or light waterproof grease. Dielectric grease, available at auto-parts stores, is even better. Spreading this grease on the surfaces will help prevent oxidation.

Melt solder around all of your wire-to-wire splices, and then coat them with liquid electrical tape or marine-grade, heat-shrink tubing to seal out dirt and water. Don't allow the trailer wiring or plug to scrape on the ground. Even if you're careful, connectors will always need occasional cleaning.

In a pinch, a few in-and-out, twisting motions with the pronged (male) part of the connector will free the female end of light corrosion. Better yet, periodically clean the prongs with a wire brush or sandpaper. Remove any deposits in the connector holes with an ice pick, a rat-tail file, or a small piece of sandpaper rolled around a toothpick. Just be sure the lights are off, or you could blow a fuse.

Alternately, electrical contact cleaner will do the job. While you're at it, clean the insides of your vehicle's plug receptacle too. Add a dab of dielectric grease to ward off corrosion. Between uses, keep both halves of the plug protected from weather and scuffing. You may wish to slip a small plastic bag over each half of the connector and secure it with a rubber band.

Here's a great tip for boat owners: Before you launch or retrieve your boat, disconnect the trailer wiring. Disconnecting will prevent problems with the light fixtures or bulbs ingesting moisture or blowing out when a hot bulb is suddenly immersed in cool water. Although a bulb change

Here, some flat aluminum stock was bent to protect the light. Also notice how a grommet is used to protect the wiring.

may not seem like a major catastrophe, you'll have to replace the entire assembly if the taillights are sealed units (such as the newer LED models). Plus, you won't have trailer lights while returning home, which is both dangerous and illegal.

BASIC ELECTRICAL TOOLS

The Volt-Ohm Meter

Digital volt-ohm meters (VOM) are so inexpensive that it's crazy to not carry one in your toolbox. Once you get used to using a VOM, troubleshooting goes much more quickly. A good volt-ohm meter, available at any electronics store, will perform specific voltage and resistance tests. A digital meter is easier to read than an analog meter.

You don't need a fancy VOM. A basic unit that costs less than one of your LED turn signals will do nicely and should be easy to use. Use a VOM to check your truck's connector for 12 volts between the ground pin and the brown wire pin (at the opposite end of the plug). Make sure the truck's parking lights are on. If that works, the problem is in the trailer wiring, and it might be worth cutting off the existing connector and attaching a new one. Also, check to see if there are any wire nuts or connectors elsewhere in the trailer wiring that may be bad.

With a VOM, you'll usually be checking for resistance. You need to know if the electricity can actually get from point A to point B. Remember that greater resistance means that you have a problem someplace in the wire or a problem with a connection.

The Basic Test Light

You'll need a basic 12-volt test light. This test light looks like a screwdriver with a pointed end and a long wire with a clip on the end. It has a bulb in the handle that will light up if there is power present. The point must be sharp enough to penetrate the insulation of a wire and thin enough to probe a connector. It can be used to check power and ground circuits.

To use the test light, connect the clip to a good ground, and then probe the terminal in question. If there's power, the bulb will light up. When you use a test light to check for ground, connect the clip to a power source (a positive battery terminal, for example), and touch the probe to the ground. If the ground is good, the bulb will light up.

Wire Strippers

Wire strippers operate like scissors, with a center notch that makes it possible to cut the insulation off a wire without cutting the actual wire. Since the insulation isn't bonded to the wire, you can simply pull it off the wire. The device has several holes that allow you to strip a variety of different wire gauges. Wire strippers range in price from about $5 to $30. Since you're only going to buy one in your lifetime, you might as well get a good wire stripper that feels comfortable in your hands.

Long Jumper Leads

Quality jumper wires are good to have on hand. You can buy them pre-made in different lengths with the clips. Instead, I buy a package of clips with screws on the wire end and use wire that I have accumulated to make them whatever length I need. Long jumper wires are great for bypassing a section of your wiring harness to help isolate a problem.

Dielectric Grease

Always have a tube of dielectric grease in your toolbox. Dielectric grease is used primarily to keep moisture out of a connection. Preventing moisture improves the ability of the connector to conduct electricity. You should use dielectric grease on all of your electrical connections and even on your battery terminals.

Once you start using dielectric grease, you'll also use it on the spark plug terminals of your tow vehicle. Dielectric grease helps prevent electrical failures caused by corrosion and moisture. Its water-resistant formulation sheds moisture and will not wash away. Available at big-box retailers and auto-parts stores, dielectric grease effectively protects bulbs, sockets, and trailer plugs.

LED VERSUS CONVENTIONAL LIGHTS

There are two styles of trailer lights: conventional incandescent bulbs and newer light-emitting diode (LED) lights. Replacement bulbs for conventional lights are inexpensive and readily available. On the other hand, LED lights have a longer bulb lifespan, look great, and react to brake light input a few milliseconds faster. But because most LED lights are sealed units, the entire unit, not just the bulb, has to be replaced when a light goes out.

Over time, LED light systems will most likely replace conventional incandescent lamps. LED lights will last longer, burn brighter, use less power, and fail less often than your normal incandescent trailer lights. Compared to conventional incandescent lamps, LED lamps last 100 times longer,

generate less heat, are more resistant to shock damage, are brighter, and have faster lighting response. The sealed acrylic lens and housing ensure maximum life expectancy for LED lamps. LED lights are great for all utility trailers, snowmobile trailers, horse trailers, car haulers, and trucks.

An LED is a solid-state device, meaning there are no fragile filaments, as in a traditional bulb. The LED lasts longer because there are no parts to weaken and eventually break. The center of an LED light is a diode mounted and held in place by a steel-lead frame, which is then encapsulated with epoxy.

A regular incandescent bulb will last around 1,000 hours, a fluorescent around 10,000 hours, and an LED around 100,000 hours. That's an incredible difference in longevity. In fact, an LED light may outlast your trailer.

LEDs draw a fraction of the power drawn by incandescent lights. If you leave your trailer lights on by mistake, you have a much better chance of starting your vehicle without a jump start than you would if you had regular lightbulbs.

LED lights are constructed as sealed units, so they can be submerged in water. LED lights are ideal for wet environments, including boat trailers.

SOME ADDITIONAL TRAILER WIRING ISSUES

Converters

Imported and some domestic tow vehicles use an international lighting system where the turn signals are separate from the brake lights. An amber lens is used for the turn signals and a red lens is used for the brake lights. The American lighting system combines the turn signals and brake lights into one wire instead of two and has no amber lens.

If your tow vehicle uses the international lighting system, then the two separate wires for turn signals and brake lights on the tow vehicle will need to be combined into one. You will need a converter for the trailer's lighting system to work properly. A converter uses a circuit board housed in either a small, waterproof box or directly inside a connector. The connector housing is preferable due to its simplicity—there's no box to mount or additional wiring to hook up. Usually, three or four wires coming from the tow vehicle (left and right turn signals, plus brake wires) go into the converter, and two come out. The two wires coming out are then attached to the left and right turn connectors in the trailer-plug receptacle.

Other Lights and Circuits

Some larger trailers have a circuit for clearance or marker lights, which are separate from the lights in the taillamp assemblies. You may need to add another circuit to handle these lights. If you try to wire them in parallel with the customary pair of running lamps, you could overload the vehicle's headlamp switch. You'll need to add a relay to handle the extra current.

This is a conventional light, meaning non-LED, mounted in a gasket.

LED lights will soon become the standard of the trailer industry.

Here's an interesting example of LED strip lighting.

Lights inside the Trailer

There may be a 12-volt circuit for the operation of lights inside the trailer or for charging the trailer battery in the case of a travel trailer. This circuit probably will be hot whenever the engine is running, but a switch on the dash might be used to control it. Be sure the wire gauge is large enough to handle the load (a fully discharged deep-cycle trailer battery may draw 20 or more amps when you start the engine). Use a battery isolator to prevent discharging the vehicle battery from the trailer and to prevent surges of current from overcooking the wiring or blowing a fuse.

Splices and Connections

Blinking or dim trailer lights are most likely caused by a bad connection. Automotive-style crimp connectors are not designed for the vibration and moisture that trailers are often exposed to.

Any crimp connect exposed to the elements will have a short lifespan. Household-style wire nuts can unscrew themselves within a few hundred miles. For your trailer, use nothing less than the screw-in posi-lock connectors.

Wiring a trailer may not be the simplest thing you've ever done, but if you go slowly, it's not that difficult. If you're towing just for the day and don't plan to tow a trailer again, you can pick up some adapters that replace the taillight bulbs in your vehicle and have pigtailed wires hanging from them.
continued on page 124

Because these are three separate lights, you'll need to run wires to each fixture.

These three separate lights serve the same purpose as a light strip. But everything is flush with the rear crossmember in this arrangement.

Light strips are becoming very popular. You only need to run one wire to this unit, and it's held in place by two screws.

continued from page 122

The way in which you route the wires from the light sockets and down to the hitch can be problematic.

Odds are the trailer and tow vehicle use different connectors; the trailer industry uses at least four styles. If you only plan on using a trailer one time, you're probably renting it. In that case the trailer rental place can hook up your wiring for you.

GENERAL TIPS TO PROLONG YOUR LIGHTING

Never use a test probe to pierce wire insulation. When you're troubleshooting lighting problems, avoid piercing the wire insulation. The hole you make will allow a wicking action that causes moisture to travel along the wire strands and corrode critical connections.

A special tool called a wire piercing lead comes with a pair of test leads. With this tool, you won't have to hold a wire in your hand and risk poking a hole in your finger. It costs $25 to $50, and the more expensive ones work best.

If probing a harness or wire is unavoidable (and sometimes it is), make sure the puncture is properly sealed. The usual RTV (room temperature vulcanizing) silicone may contain an acid, so it's best to use a dielectric silicone or liquid electrical tape. This product comes in either a clear or black formulation and is available at most hardware stores.

To correct voltage problems, look for the cause. Low voltage is often caused by poor electrical connections. To correct undervoltage or illumination problems, find out what's causing the voltage problem. Don't assume anything when solving lamp problems; explore all avenues to make sure you identify the true source of a problem rather than simply fixing a symptom of a greater problem.

If you have conventional lights, open the lens and examine the bulb. The bulb will help tell you what failed. For example:

- A bulb with stretched or broken filaments was subjected to heavy vibration.
- A yellowish, whitish, or bluish glaze on the bulb indicates a rupture in the bulb glass envelope and a possible leak.
- A dark, metallic finish indicates old age.
- A black, sooty bulb indicates a poor seal in the bulb.

All bulbs will last longer if they're kept cool. Because dirt on the lens increases the heat, you should keep the lens as clean as possible. The purpose of the lighting system is to let people see your trailer, and clean lenses also allow other people to see your lights. Heat is one of the most damaging conditions for a standard incandescent bulb. A cluster of LEDs can also be damaged by heat. Interestingly, aluminum light housings offer significant heat benefits over the plastic housing, as the anodized aluminum dissipates the heat into the trailer body. All lighting must breathe to eliminate the damage from heat buildup.

Treat the electrical system the same way you treat the chassis—lube it. Lubricate all of the sockets, pigtails, battery

The separate grounding wire is placed under one of the mounting bolts in such a way that the terminal teeth dig through the paint and into the frame of the trailer.

terminals, and connections with dielectric grease. This grease encapsulates the connection and protects it against corrosion and water. Don't use sodium-based greases, as the sodium will emulsify if it ever comes in contact with water.

Always check for bad ground connections. Bad grounds are a major cause of bulb failure. When lights are grounded through the lamp housing, make sure that there's a clean metal-to-metal connection. Also, keep in mind that this type of grounding is the cheapest method but not the best idea.

Look for loose, bare, and unsupported wires. The wiring harnesses should be placed on the frame members wherever possible rather than on the bottom where dirt and road splash collect.

Always replace trailer wiring with wire that is at least equal, or heavier, than the original wire. If you use lighter-gauge wire, you can cause unnecessary problems. Wire has certain resistance to current flow. The smaller the wire, the greater the resistance will be. Wire is inexpensive and not a sensible place to cut costs.

Check the rubber grommets that house the trailer lights. As rubber grommets age, they deteriorate from exposure to sunlight, ozone, and harmful chemicals. New grommets will restore shock protection and make your trailer look a lot nicer.

SOME BASIC WIRING ISSUES

Corrosion

Problem: Corrosion is the result of water, dirt, and other environmental elements from the road and surrounding

Again, you will want to make sure that grommets protect the wires as they pass through the frame of the trailer. Road vibrations will cause the wires to rub against whatever they are touching. So you want them touching something soft and nonconductive.

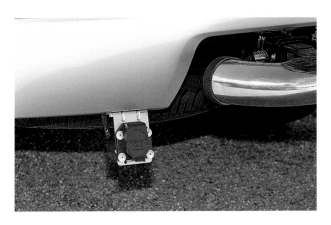

This receptacle is riveted to the bracket. I prefer bolts with Nylock nuts in this application. If you have to replace this plug, you'll have to drill out the rivet heads.

conditions. Corrosion takes a while to develop and usually attacks your trailer wiring at several different points.

Solutions: Corrosion around the bulb sockets can't attack the bulb when it's sealed within a quality lamp housing. In a cheap lamp housing, there's very little protection against the elements. Whatever money you save on these cheap lights you'll end up paying for several times over in troubleshooting time. To further protect against corrosion, all electrical wiring connections should be sealed against moisture with dielectric grease or another nonconductive, non-sodium-based grease. Areas such as electrical contacts, circuit switches, and junction boxes should be sealed.

Filament Damage from Shock and Vibration

Problem: When traveling down the highway, the trailer is subjected to constant road pounding. This shock and vibration causes filaments in the bulb to weaken and break prematurely, which ends in a burned-out bulb.

This is a simple, yet elegant way to run wires from the front to the rear of the trailer. It looks as if the manufacturer welded a washer into place and then installed a grommet to protect the wires.

Solutions: You can install lights with a shock-mounted mechanism that cradles the bulb and absorbs the effects of shock and vibration that otherwise would be transferred directly to fragile bulb filaments. The best way to eliminate shock and filament vibration is to upgrade to a complete LED lighting system. You won't reduce the amount of shock that your bulbs encounter, but you'll eliminate all of your filament concerns.

Inadequate Wiring and Cable

Problem: After a few years of cutting and splicing, or merging various harnesses and wiring systems that aren't designed to work together, you'll break down the electrical system's modularity.

Solutions: Remember that a larger-gauge wire can be used in any circuit for very little additional cost while at the same time offering reliable results. Also, the quality of the wire is very important. Stranded copper wire, which has a greater capacity to conduct electricity, should be used throughout your trailer lighting system. Galvanic action can form oxides at crimp connections with aluminum wire, limiting the ability of the wire to carry current. Copper wire resists heat better than aluminum wire, thereby reducing the number of problems.

Poor Grounding

Problem: There are two major causes of grounding problems. First, the ground contact is open to the elements. Rain, sleet, and snow can cause corrosion that will eventually eliminate the actual contact. Second, the screws that hold the ground wire to the trailer may simply come loose.

Solutions: On most trailers, the ground wire is the white wire, and it's attached to the trailer with a sheetmetal screw. For a quick test of the grounding wire, run a separate ground wire from the chassis of the tow vehicle to the chassis of the trailer. If everything works when you do this, you absolutely have a bad ground.

WIRE COLOR BY VEHICLE MANUFACTURER

Dual-Purpose Bulb System

Wire Function	Trailer Wire Color	GMC	Ford	Chrysler	Jeep	Toyota	Honda	Mazda
Right turn & brake lights	Green	Green	Orange w/ blue stripe	Brown	Brown	Green w/ yellow stripe	Green w/ yellow stripe	Green w/ yellow stripe
Left turn & brake lights	Yellow	Yellow	Light green w/orange stripe	Dark green	Gray w/ black stripe	Green w/ blue stripe	Green w/ black stripe	Black stripe
Taillights	Brown	Brown	Brown	Black w/ yellow stripe or black	Blue	Red w/ green stripe	Red w/ black stripe	Green or black stripe
Ground	White	Black	Black or gray	Black	Black and black	Black or white	Black	Black

Single-Purpose Bulb System

Brake lights	Use converter	Pink or light blue	Red w/ green stripe	White	Blue w/ black stripe	Green w/ red or white stripe	Green w/ white stripe	Green or green w/ red stripe
Backup lights	Red	Light green	Black w/ pink	Violet	Brown	-	-	-
Electric trailer brakes	Connect to blue wire from brake controller							

Note: Vehicle manufacturers have changed wiring colors over the years. I recommend that you use a circuit tester on the tow vehicle's wiring harness to verify that you've located the correct wire. This chart is designed only to give you a place to start.

If you still have lighting problems, start tracing wires, especially anywhere they've been cut or spliced. As you go along, replace all connections while you're checking that they're hooked up correctly. When all else fails, rewire the whole trailer. It may be quicker than spending endless hours troubleshooting.

Poor Bulb Contact

Problem: In the traditional S-8 non-shock-mounted bulb units and the standard J-slot bulb socket, loss of contact is generally caused by corrosion or lack of the spring tension that should hold the bulb in place.

Solution: To solve poor bulb contact once and for all, switch to LED technology, which has no bulbs, no filaments, and no internal wiring connections and is completely sealed. The other solution is to replace the socket that's giving you the problem.

Plastic is now the standard for brackets. This license-plate bracket will never rust and it won't bend. It comes pre-drilled for all the necessary lights.

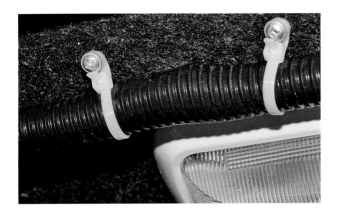

You have to support any wiring used in your trailer. Tie-wraps are available is a variety of configurations.

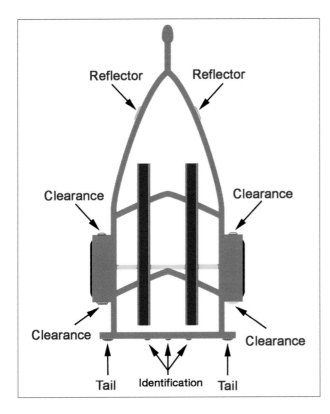

Reflector   Reflector

Clearance   Clearance

Clearance   Clearance

Tail   Identification   Tail

These are the federal requirements for any trailer less than 80 inches wide.

Physical Damage

Problem: Physical damage can take several forms. First, there may be no protection for a light placed in a vulnerable area. Lenses break easily. Second, bulb heat builds up with no method to dissipate it. In both cases, the problem may be cheaply made plastic light housings.

Solutions: To solve both problems, use a supertough, high-impact plastic that's impervious to heat generated by the bulb and to physical damage from typical use. Lexan lenses offer additional security against physical damage. Both lenses and lamp housings should be made of tough plastic.

In addition, try to use recessed mounts to protect the lights from impact damage. An anodized aluminum housing found on some lights will allow any heat to dissipate into the trailer frame.

Excessive Voltage

Problem: Excessive voltage is always a difficult problem for bulb life. Some people claim that as many as 60 percent of bulb failures are not as they appear. The true reason for all these bulb failures is problems in the wiring system, either due to poor grounding or a problem inherent to the electrical system itself that has produced a voltage surge and affected the lighting system.

Solutions: Check the voltage regularly to ensure the vehicle is operating within a safe range. Remember that only 1 volt beyond the designed voltage is enough to reduce the expected life of a bulb filament by more than half. You may also try to reduce the overall power consumption of your electrical system by installing an LED lighting system.

TRAILER WIRING FAQS

Q: Why am I constantly blowing fuses in my tow vehicle?

A: First, check all your wires for bare copper or places where a wire could be pinched and touching metal on both the trailer or the tow vehicle's chassis. If that's not the problem, then calculate the amp load your trailer is pulling. Most vehicles are equipped to handle only standard lighting on trailers—that is, one turn/brake signal light on each side and one marker light on each front corner. Check your vehicle owner's manual for specific power ratings. If it's not a short or a pinched wire and your vehicle is rated to supply the necessary number of amps (power), then it's time to find a good electrical shop.

Q: Should I unplug my boat trailer when I back my boat into the water?

A: Yes. Always unplug your boat trailer when backing into the water. When the trailer lights are submerged, it can create a short that causes vehicle fuses to blow. If you have sealed lights, however, this is unnecessary. All boat trailer lights since the early 1990s have been sealed, some more effectively than others. If the lights are submersible units, the packaging will usually state this in great big letters.

Q: When I have my headlights on and apply the brakes, all the lights on my trailer go out. What causes this?

A: You have a ground problem that's strong enough to provide some lighting functions but not all. This is called a weak ground. When the taillights and brake lights are used at the same time, it creates the maximum amperage load on the trailer. If a ground problem exists, it will show up at this point. The places to check grounds are as follows:

• The connector on the tow vehicle should have a ground wire secured tightly to a clean surface on the frame. A wire attached to the body or a surface with undercoating,

BASIC LIGHTING ISSUES

If you have chronic trailer light problems and your current lights look beat up, you might want to replace the entire mess. Lights are inexpensive and take little time to install; it's foolish to keep messing around with connections and testing for continuity. A new lighting kit with a wiring harness for your utility trailer can cost under $50 and can be installed in a few hours. Besides, it gets you out of the house on a Saturday morning.

It can be difficult to run wires through box-section trailer frames, so you may want to pull a messenger through before yanking the old wires completely out. Each trailer will present new and unique challenges, so work slowly.

- Color-coding is simple. The white wire is generally the ground wire. Even though the trailer hitch acts as a ground, you should always connect the white wire to the vehicle ground and the trailer frame. The brown wire is for taillights and runs to both the red lights in the back and to the clearance lights. The green wire is for the right-turn indicator, and the yellow wire is for the left-turn indicator.
- European, Japanese, and some American vehicles use separate circuits for turn signals and brake lights. If your vehicle uses amber rear turn indicators or uses a different area of its light fixture for turning than for braking, you'll need a five-wire to four-wire converter. These converters are relatively cheap and can be a permanent part of the tow vehicle wiring harness.
- The two most common ways to blow out trailer lights are immersing a hot bulb in cold water or letting corrosion create a short. Remember to disconnect trailer lights before launching a boat. Be sure the connector plug to the car doesn't touch the water.

- It's possible to force bayonet lamps such as #1157 into their sockets reversed. If this happens, the bright and dim filaments will come on at the wrong time. Be sure to always get the bulb guides in the right slots, and don't force them in. If it seems hard to install the new bulb, stop and look at what you're doing.
- Use only stranded wire on your trailer. It's more flexible and chafe resistant than solid wire.
- Secure any exposed wires with wire ties every 18 inches to prevent chafing, and use rubber grommets to protect the insulation when you run wires through trailer frame holes. Inspect the entire system twice a year for bare or chafed wire, and give all of the contacts a protective dab of dielectric grease.
- If you use light assemblies with replaceable bulbs, keep several replacement bulbs in your traveling toolbox. You'll be glad you did when you burn out a lamp in West B'Gosh at o'dark-thirty.

paint, or rust can cause a ground problem. All ground wires should be metal-to-metal.
- The ground connector on the trailer should have a wire running from the connector to a tightly secured clean surface on the trailer.
- Each taillamp assembly at the back of the trailer must also be grounded. This is done in one of two ways: First, a separate wire comes from the back of each taillamp assembly and is properly secured to the frame. Second, ground is achieved through the bolts of the taillamp assembly. In this case, the lamp housing must be attached to the frame of the trailer. If the lights are mounted on wood or PVC material, the lights will not get a ground.
- The last possibility to explore is in the trailer design. If the trailer has a tilting bed, it's very possible the ground isn't passing through the pivot point, resulting in a poor ground. Try routing a ground wire from the connector at the front of the trailer to each lamp assembly at the back of the trailer, bypassing the pivot point. It's a little

complicated, but it'll solve the problem. Remember that the trailer hitch and ball connection area should never be considered sufficient ground.

Q: When I use one turn signal, why does the other one blink?

A: This is usually related to one of two things: There could be a short somewhere in the system. Check and test all wiring and the vehicle connector. The second and most common cause is a weak ground somewhere in the system.

Q: When my trailer is connected to my vehicle, the turn signals are dim and flash rapidly. What's the problem?

A: When you add trailer lights to a vehicle system, the turn-signal amp load basically doubles. Older vehicles have a flasher unit that controls the blinking of a turn signal. The standard flasher provided in many vehicles can't handle this extra load. This flasher is often located under the dashboard. On newer vehicles, it's connected to the fuse box and simply pulls out. There are usually two flasher modules, one flasher for the turn signals and one for the four-way emergency lights. You should only need to

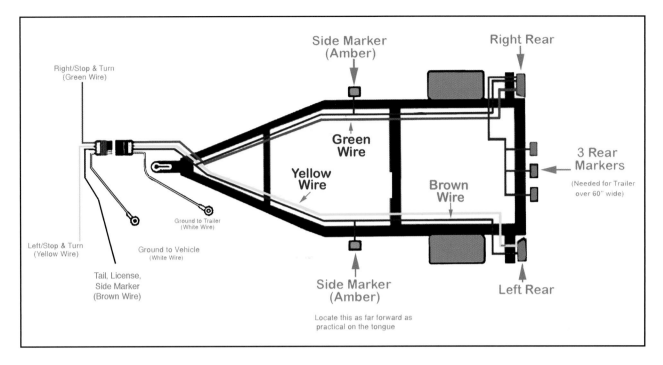

This is a lighting diagram for a boat trailer. Any trailer less than 80 inches wide should be lit the same way.

replace the turn-signal flasher module. Replace the basic flasher unit with a heavy-duty flasher (8 to 10 amps), and make sure the vehicle engine is running when you test the lights. The heavy-duty flasher unit will slow down your turn signals, and a running engine will increase the brightness of the lamps.

LIGHTS AND THE LAW

The legal requirements for trailer lights can be grouped into two classes: trailers less than 80 inches wide and trailers more than 80 inches wide. Trailers less than 80 inches wide are required to have taillights, stop lights, turn signals, side marker lights, and side and rear reflectors on each side. Most states also require a license plate light.

Trailers that are *over* 80 inches wide need a few additional lights to help define the perimeter of the trailer. At the rear of these wide trailers, three red identification lights are required. You can usually buy these as a single bar with the lights mounted at the required spacing. They look a lot like the top of a tractor-trailer rig and the rear of its trailer.

Clearance lights, intended to alert drivers to the width of your trailer, are generally required on each side of trailers over 89 inches wide and should be placed as far outboard as possible (generally on the trailer fenders).

CHAPTER 11
TRAILER ACCESSORIES

COMPONENTS COUNT

Many components used on a trailer will contribute to its strength or weakness. The quality of these components is a good indication of shortcuts or cheapness in the design of your trailer. Here are a few things to look at before making a purchase.

The Hitch Ball

The ball receiver and hitch should be appropriately sized for the trailer capacity. Both the ball and the receiver should have a load capacity stamped on them. That capacity should be at *least* 15 percent of the loaded trailer weight. In other words, if your loaded trailer weighs 5,000 pounds, the hitch ball should have a capacity of at least 750 pounds. This isn't too difficult since companies such as Reese Hitches actually give you a gross trailer weight (GTW) capacity for each hitch ball they sell. All you have to do is pay attention to what they tell you.

The ball receiver should be made for a ball of adequate size. In general, the ball should be at least 1 7/8 inches ball diameter for trailers of a 2,000-pound capacity, and at least 2 inches ball diameter for trailers of a 3,500-pound capacity. When you get into the really heavy-duty trailers, you'll find hitch balls of 2 5/16 inches diameter. The simple solution to all of this is to match the hitch ball to the weight class of your trailer hitch. If that's too hard for you, just stop at the local trailer store for suggestions.

You really need to know four things when you purchase a hitch ball: the thickness of the ball platform, the size of the hole in the platform, your gross trailer weight, and the size of the trailer coupler socket. These four things will determine which hitch ball you're going to buy.

Hitch balls come in a variety of finishes, but that doesn't mean much when it comes to strength. Chrome and zinc hitch balls are usually about the same price. The stainless-steel balls are more than double the price of a chrome ball. I prefer the stainless hitch balls just because I know the finish won't flake off. On the other hand, zinc plating works just fine for most people.

Also, make sure the trailer hitch on the vehicle matches the intended use. A lot of the newer SUVs come with small receivers, which limit the towing capacity. The manufacturers do that specifically to limit the size of the trailer you can pull. Pay attention to the limits of your vehicle.

Trailer Couplers

The coupler may be the most important part of your towing mechanism, although it's rarely given much thought. The trailer coupler is the connection point that ties the trailer to the vehicle. It's what allows you to attach your trailer to the tow vehicle. The coupler must be of good quality and meet the load-capacity requirements of your cargo. There are two basic types of couplers used on our trailers: straight couplers and A-frame couplers. The type of trailer you're towing will determine the type of coupler that meets your needs. Remember that the basic purpose of any coupler is to secure the towing vehicle to the trailer.

Straight Couplers

Straight couplers are most often found on utility and small boat trailers that don't require a tongue jacking system. Some small utility trailers even use a folding coupler on which the tongue actually folds back on itself to give you about 2 feet of extra clearance when you store the trailer.

A-Frame Couplers

A-frame couplers are generally found on trailers that require a hefty jacking system. Large utility trailers, boat or horse trailers, and even large motorcycle trailers usually use A-frame couplers.

The standard A-frame coupler has a 50-degree angle and can be either welded or bolted into place. A-frame couplers are also available for both Class 3 and Class 4 towing rigs. I prefer the bolted units because they can be easily replaced if they are damaged.

Maintaining Your Trailer Coupler

The trailer coupler is the most abused part of any trailer. It's often run over, jackknifed, bent, or somehow broken. To ensure longer coupler life, always make sure the latching mechanism is secure and that the coupler is the right size for the ball.

Occasionally, you should check that the welds or bolts holding the coupler to the trailer tongue are secure. Make sure you have quality bolts with adequate strength.

In addition, clean and lubricate the latching mechanism regularly. This mechanism secures your trailer to your vehicle; therefore, it's important that it's not rusted to the point of falling apart. You should never have to beat the locking mechanism into place with a block of wood. Take some time to coat the ball socket and clamping face with chassis grease. Periodically oil all of the pivot points and sliding surfaces of the coupler.

When you park or store your trailer, keep the coupler off the ground so dirt doesn't build up in the ball socket. Too many people simply let the trailer tongue lie on the ground. Using the tongue jack can protect your coupler.

When you get ready to pull out of the driveway, make sure the coupler is secured to the hitch ball and the lock lever is fully engaged. If your trailer uses a hand wheel, make sure it's down tight and locked. Wheel couplers should be hand tight only. Always check to make sure that the ball clamp is properly nested under the ball and not sitting on top of the ball. At the first rest stop, do this all over again.

Safety Chains

Safety chains are not optional. They're required in most places and are a very good idea. The chains (and the chain attachment points on both the trailer and the tow vehicle) must be of an appropriate size for the trailer. Obviously, a small, light-duty trailer needs far less in a safety chain than a Caterpillar-hauling monster trailer.

There are a couple of ways to hook safety chains to your tow vehicle. I often use simple S-hooks, because they are fast and easy, but I do not recommend them. Quick Links—those little threaded oval things—are probably a better idea. It's even better to use a Clevis Slip Hook that has a positive locking mechanism on the hook.

There is a standardized grading system for chains. Most of the trailer safety chains are Grade 30 and are made of low-carbon steel. This general utility chain is intended for rather basic applications. The next step up is Grade 40, which has higher tensile strength and resistance to wear compared to the Grade 30. If you can locate a Grade 40 safety chain, it might be a nice upgrade, but don't go out of your way looking for it.

TONGUE JACKS

Almost every trailer has a tongue jack. A new trailer often comes with the cheapest possible unit, yet the tongue jack is one place where spending money can make a huge difference. Trailer jacks are designed to ease the loading and unloading of the trailer from the hitch ball of the tow vehicle. The tongue jack can also be used to raise your trailer to a proper storage angle. Some tongue jacks have a tongue that telescopes into itself, while others have a tongue that folds up into a horizontal position.

Tongue jacks are available with a wheel or a flat steel foot. The size of the tongue jack wheel or plate determines how easy it is to move the trailer around. You'll benefit from a wheeled tongue jack on a small, single-axle trailer, since these trailers are small enough to wheel around by hand. As long as you're on a firm surface, the small jack wheels work nicely;

This impressive tongue jack is powered by a 12-volt battery.

This tongue jack is centered on the tongue, rather than on the side of the tongue.

This simple tongue jack is effective and easy to use. If you park the trailer on soft ground or asphalt, this large foot will work better than a wheel.

but if you find yourself on gravel, dirt, or mud, you'll want a bigger wheel. If you store your trailer on dirt or grass, a large tongue jack wheel is well worth the money.

Tongue jacks are available in hand-operated or electronically operated styles. Electric tongue jacks require a power source, which can make things a little more complicated. On the other hand, if you have a large, heavy trailer, an electric tongue jack is nice to have. The most common types of jacks are A-frame jacks, swivel jacks, and drop-leg jacks.

A-Frame Jacks

A-frame jacks have triangular mounting brackets that provide an easy bolt-on or weld-on mounting system for trailers that have an A-frame-mounted coupler. Be aware that not all A-frame tongue jacks have the same load capacities. It's critical that you determine the maximum load your trailer will be carrying before you purchase an A-frame jack. I prefer to go slightly oversize to be safe.

An A-frame jack is pretty easy to install, and you usually have the choice of welding it in place or bolting it down. I prefer bolting the jack to the tongue to have the option to replace it at a later date. If you use bolts, use Grade 5 bolts rather than carriage bolts to ensure the unit's strength.

Swivel Jacks

Swivel jacks allow the jack tube to move easily from its horizontal position to a vertical, stationary position and then lock securely into place. Swivel jacks are most common on boat trailers. Once again, keep in mind that not all swivel jacks have the same load capacity. Before purchasing a swivel jack for your boat trailer, confirm the required load capacities.

Drop-Leg Jacks

Drop-leg jacks are strong, durable, and sturdy. They're most often used in agricultural, construction, heavy-duty utility, horse/livestock, and camper trailers. If you use one of these jacks, add camper stabilizer jacks for the rear undercarriage of your trailer for extra stability. A system with a drop-leg jack in the front and stabilizer jacks in the rear will make leveling the trailer much easier. As with all tongue jacks, remember that not all drop-leg jacks have the same weight capacities. Before you make a purchase, confirm your maximum trailer load.

Tips for Trailer Jacks

Before you mount your trailer jack, check for interference from recessed ball mounts, the trailer coupler, and the hitch or vehicle bumper. Rotate the jack handle to make sure that the handle isn't obstructed by any part of the towing mechanism.

If you're using a swivel jack, check the unit in both the vertical and horizontal positions. When a swivel jack is in a horizontal, or storage, position, there shouldn't be any interference from structural members of the trailer or the trailer

continued on page 134

If you look closely under the ramp on the left side of the picture, you'll see some homemade jack stands that allow the owner to back a car off this trailer without having the tongue fly up into the air. Notice the array of tie-down clamps across the rear of this trailer.

Electric winches are wonderful for both loading and unloading cargo. With a winch, you can slowly lower a car off the trailer without using a series of chocks to get it down the ramp slowly.

Roof ladders are wonderful if you intend to store items on the roof of your trailer.

CHOOSING THE CORRECT BALL MOUNT

Remember that the trailer should always be as level as possible. A level trailer puts less strain on the connection between the trailer and tow vehicle. It will also help the trailer stay in line behind the vehicle.

Since trailer and vehicle heights often differ, a ball mount with a rise or a drop may be needed. To determine how much of a rise or drop you need, follow the simple steps below.

1. Measure the hitch height—the height from the ground to the top of the receiver opening on the trailer hitch. With the tow vehicle parked on level ground, measure to the top of the 2-inch hole on Class 3 and Class 4 hitches. On Class 5 hitches, the receiver opening will be 2 1/2 inches, but you still measure to the top of the hole.

2. Now measure the coupler height—the distance from the ground to the bottom of the trailer's coupler. Check to make sure the trailer is level and on level ground.

3. Now compute the difference between the hitch height and the coupler height. If the hitch height is greater than the coupler height, the difference is the drop that is required. If the coupler height is greater, the difference is the rise that is required. Select the ball mount with the rise or drop closest to the difference.

For example, let's say the hitch height equals 17 inches, and the coupler height equals 15 inches. Because the hitch height is greater, a ball mount with a drop of 2 inches will be required to level the trailer. Ball mounts with 2 inches of drop are common and the best choice for this scenario.

continued from page 132

coupler. Also, make certain that the swivel jack doesn't come in contact with the tow vehicle when you make a tight turn. On all jacks, check that you have adequate ground clearance to drive down the road.

When you're cranking the jack or coupling the trailer to the hitch, secure the trailer from rolling with blocks on both sides. These trailer jacks are designed only for vertical loading; any side forces should be avoided. When using an optional footplate or caster, always remove the footplate, or the wheel, before towing. If you have a swivel jack, remember to raise this jack to its storage position before you begin towing.

OPTIONAL STRUCTURES

Sides

The sides on a utility trailer come in all different sizes and configurations. Think about your intended use, and then choose sides or not. The sides can be permanent or removable, solid or slatted, tall or short. If you decide you want sides, you may also want a trailer top, which can be canvas or hard, and permanent or removable. A top may lift to gain access, or it may be stationary. Tops are found most often on snowmobile trailers.

Fenders

There are all sorts of fenders available, from stamped steel or plastic to fiberglass or wood. They come as square, round, or even something called Shipshape for your boat trailer. They all essentially do the same job, so looks and taste are the biggest considerations. Check your state laws for fender requirements.

There's no federal requirement regarding trailer fenders. There is, however, an SAE (Society of Automotive

Awnings are nice.

Engineers) recommended practice standard (J682) that says that mud flaps are required if the ratio of the bottom of the trailer bed to the length from the bottom of the wheel to the end of the trailer is greater than 1:3. In other words, if the bottom of the frame, at the end of the trailer is, say, 25 inches, then the center of the rear wheels must be more than 75 inches from the back of the trailer. If it is less than 75 inches, then you need flaps of a length to restrict the ratio to the 1:3 number. All of this is so confusing that only trailer manufacturers need to be concerned with the issue. If we don't get it, and there are no laws regarding this ratio, then you're most likely not going to get a ticket from a local police officer.

Ramps

On some trailers, the ramp is actually a tailgate that folds down. Sometimes these are purpose-built for motorcycles or ATVs. I like the ramp systems that allow you to store the ramp under the deck of the trailer. Think a lot about what type of ramp system will work best for you.

Tie-Down Points

Tie-down points are especially important with open utility trailers. The tie points may be part of the frame, or they may be attached to the sides. Examine the standard tie points to be sure they're adequate, accessible, and not in the way. Tie points should be located in convenient places for the intended loads or have adjustable positioning. Dedicated tie points for specific loads (such as motorcycles or ATVs) should be strong enough for the given application.

E-tracks

E-tracks comprise a very versatile tie-down system. They can be surface-mounted or recessed into walls and floors and allow almost unlimited tie-down locations. E-tracks are especially great if you haul a variety of equipment that may change from time to time.

There's a huge variety of accessories available for the E-track systems. There are also a number of E-track systems available for motorcycles. The best part is that this versatile tie-down system won't cost much more than a fixed tie-down system.

If you haul race cars around, you also haul tires. This tire rack is an accessory offered by the trailer manufacturer. It fits and is easy to remove, making the trailer more versatile.

This auxiliary step folds back into the trailer.

Side doors can be a wonderful convenience.

The rollers on the back of this trailer protect the trailer in the event it makes contact with the ground during travel.

If you haul cars around, you know you often can't open the car doors with fenders installed. Removable fenders with spring-loaded latches allow the best of both worlds.

D-rings

D-rings mount on the deck of your trailer and are available in various weight ratings and sizes. D-rings are the most common way to tie down cargo. If you'll always be hauling the same item, such as a race car, D-rings may be the way to go. What they lack in versatility they make up for in ease of use.

Storage Compartments

Compartments such as a tongue box can make a nice addition to a trailer. Make certain that any storage box you purchase has a weather-tight seal. You may put tools, tie-downs, and other items in these useful storage boxes. Utility boxes can also be added to the sides just in front of or behind the wheels, or even under the trailer bed. Placement depends on the specific application and your needs.

Nose Cones

Enclosed trailers or large RV trailers that come equipped with nose cones cost a little more at the onset but are less expensive to tow. Your trailer will be affected less by changes in wind conditions, and your gas mileage will improve. The nose cone allows for a safer, more comfortable drive with better fuel economy. They won't solve the global warming problem, but you get the idea.

Big flat-front trailers increase what the engine perceives as load weight. If the trailer is loaded to the maximum towing capacity, the boxy trailer itself could put the load over *continued on page 142*

Featherlite incorporates many nice features into its trailers. These ramps slide directly into a compartment in the trailer.

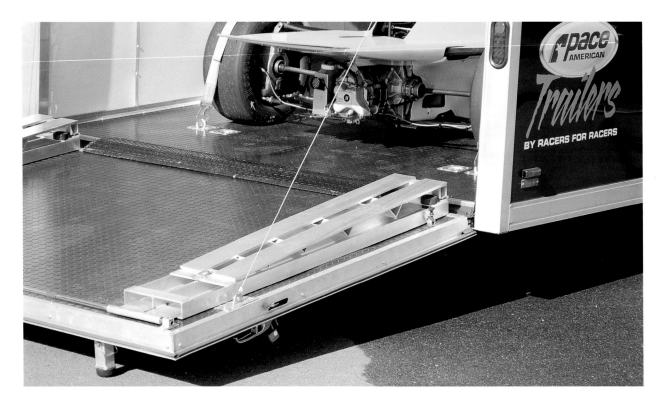

These ramps not only fold back on themselves for easy storage, but also slide along the rod you see in the picture. Notice the multiple tie-down points behind the race car.

The stock trailer ramps never seem to be long enough for unloading a race car. Race cars are so low to the ground that they require a very small angle. These Race Ramps extend the length of the ramps, thus changing the angle.

Several long pieces of angle iron, a cutting device, and a welder are enough to create strong homemade ramps.

These versatile tie-downs not only lie flat when not in use, but also swivel.

This welded tie-down is very strong, but lacks versatility.

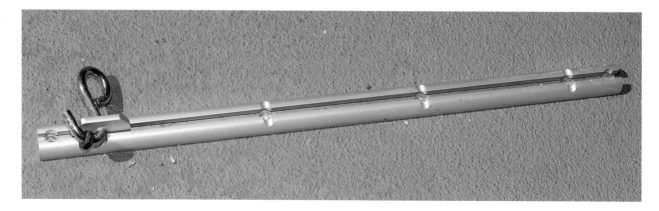

This version of the old E-track system is made of anodized aluminum and used in a toy box trailer.

Side-mounted toolboxes are one solution to storage problems.

The floor and cabinets on this trailer were designed to be easy to keep clean.

continued from page 137

capacity, increasing the strain on the tow vehicle's engine, frame, and axles. For example, a typical pickup truck without a trailer requires 7 pounds of turbo boost to cruise along a level interstate at 70 to 75 miles per hour. Add an 8-foot-wide flat-front trailer with only 2,200 pounds gross weight, and manifold pressure will increase to 14 or 15 pounds to maintain the same speed. That's twice the amount of horsepower to tow only 2,200 pounds. It's not the weight but rather poor aerodynamics that increases the power costs as much as 20 percent in additional fuel. The same application with a nose cone–equipped trailer requires only 10 pounds of turbo boost, using 33 percent less power than the flat-front trailer.

With a nose cone, most people improve their mileage by about 0.5 miles per gallon. Play with your calculator to see if it's all worth it. Look at the price of fuel and how many miles you will be driving with the trailer. The nose cone won't have a quick return on investment. Then again, if gas prices continue to climb, nose cones will become more worthwhile as the payback on the initial cost is quicker.

This roof vent lets light into your trailer while allowing heat to escape.

A stabilizer jack is a wonderful feature to have for those times when you need to park on uneven ground. It allows you to level the floor of the trailer, no matter where you are parked.

This is an inexpensive and effective anti-theft device.

Keep in mind that nose cones add weight to your trailer, and this weight is up high, which may be the least desirable place for this additional weight. They're also one more thing to get damaged, and the color will fade differently from the rest of the trailer. Nonetheless, there's a benefit to nose cones, but you have to do the math to see just how much of a benefit they might be.

Air Deflectors

There are two different types of roof-mounted wind deflectors. The first type requires drilling into your vehicle's roof in order to bolt them on. The second type stands on suction-cup feet to protect the roof of your vehicle. You don't have to drill holes in your roof or modify your vehicle in any way. This second type securely fastens to your roof with four nylon straps and vinyl-coated hooks that attach between the door

and roof. This mounting method makes the wind deflector very easy to remove.

The deflectors that bolt in place are obviously much more secure, but they require that you permanently modify your tow vehicle. This could be a real problem if you lease your tow vehicle. Even if you own it, the holes could be an issue when it comes time to get a new truck.

Stone Guards

Stone guards protect the front of your trailer from rocks and other road debris. Diamond-plated aluminum seems to be the material of choice, as many trailers come standard with this diamond plate.

The type of aluminum diamond plate is a real indication of the quality of construction. Too often it's just some shiny thin sheets cut out with hand-operated shears. If you want a

Anti-theft devices are probably the most popular trailer accessories. This trailer has two in place.

Anti-theft devices don't get much cheaper or more effective than this.

Sure, you can make your own shelves, but these aluminum racks just look so much better. And they are not very expensive.

really high-quality trailer, you might consider using stainless steel that's at least 0.125 inch thick. Some people actually space the stone guards 1/4 inch off the trailer panels. This way even if the stone guard is damaged, the wall of you trailer will remain damage free.

Stabilizer Jacks

Stabilizer jacks are usually mounted to the rear of smaller trailers and allow you to load or unload your trailer without having it connected to your tow vehicle. Without a stabilizer jack, the front of your trailer could rise up when too much weight is moved to behind the axles. You

can accomplish the same thing with a couple of adjustable jack stands.

Spare Wheel/Tire

Spare tires are a necessary evil. Most trailers don't come with spares, but make sure you have one available in case you need it.

Roof/Sidewall Vents

Roof and sidewall vents allow heat and fumes to exit your trailer while you're driving down the road. Roof vents even provide ventilation while you're parked. If you park your trailer in an unshaded area, this can be a huge benefit.

You also have some choices about how the vents operate. Some of the vents use fans that are temperature controlled. Most of these units operate off a 12-volt electrical system and have three different speeds. A reversible fan is also nice to have. These units with all the bells and whistles usually run about $300.

Another item that's nice to have is a rain sensor for your vents. This type of system automatically closes the vent when the sensor gets wet. When the sensor dries out, the vents reopen. This can save you from climbing around your trailer in the rain. It's even more useful should you drive through a rainstorm on the way to your next location.

THEFT PROTECTION

Trailers are stolen every day. It happens often enough that you need to be concerned and take steps to hold on to your trailer. State Farm Insurance reported a few years ago that it paid out $200 million in theft claims. That was just for one year. That number got my attention.

The most common device is a padlock that fits through the coupler. This is cheap and pretty effective for most purposes. On the other hand, it won't even slow down a professional thief. Someone can just hitch up. Better yet, they can just bring a roll-back truck and winch your trailer onto their truck and drive away with your trailer. Here are a couple of suggestions to help prevent that:

- Store your trailer in a locked garage, a secured storage facility, or a ministorage warehouse.
- Keep the trailer inside your yard, preferably out of sight, and in your back yard.
- If possible, turn the trailer around so that it's nose in rather than out.
- In a carport or driveway, always park a vehicle in front of the trailer, blocking easy removal.
- If you store the trailer outside, remove at least one wheel from the trailer.
- Use a heavy-duty chain and lock to secure both the boat and trailer to a fixed object such as a tree or post.
- No matter how you store your trailer, get a trailer hitch lock.
- Purchase a trailer that allows you to remove the forward part of the tongue, which contains the hitch.

CHAPTER 12
BUILDING OR REBUILDING A TRAILER

The easiest way to buy a trailer is to head down to the local trailer store and write a check. The salesperson will hook it up to your tow vehicle, all of the wiring will work, and the tires will have enough air in them. This is what most reasonable people do. Then there are the rest of us. . . . Faced with the need for a trailer, we start thinking about building our own. Or we may take an old trailer and update, customize, or restore it. While some people rebuild trailers to save money, others rebuild them to demonstrate their abilities.

I've seen very few trailers that are absolute junk, because the main components of a trailer seldom wear out. While everything attached to the frame might be worthless, the main structural components of the frame itself are seldom bent or cracked.

Be aware that you may not save any money by the time you're done refurbishing or rebuilding a used trailer. When I finish rebuilding a trailer, I often have as much money tied up in it as I might have spent purchasing a new one. This situation is especially true with teardrop trailers and utility trailers.

TRAILER PLANS

A real trailer requires plans that will cost $25 to $30. If you think that's a lot of money, you really should buy a trailer that's already built. You will spend real money to build your own trailer. Exactly how much depends on factors such as your welding skills and your ability to scrounge parts. If you have access to short lengths of steel and a heavy-duty welder, you can build a trailer slightly cheaper than you could buy one. If you have to buy new steel from a steel supplier and hire someone to do the welding, you'll be very close to what it costs to simply buy a trailer from a local dealer.

I wouldn't consider building a trailer without a set of professional plans as a guideline. Modifying a set of plans is much safer than starting from a set of chalk lines on your garage floor. Plans really do help. There's a limit to backyard engineering. It's not the 1950s anymore.

THE KITS

Trailer kits are worth considering if you're intent on a do-it-yourself project. These kits let you have the fun of assembling your own trailer and allow you to save some money. They also reduce the amount of engineering you have to do when you build a trailer from scratch.

Be careful when you shop for a trailer kit, as some of them require welding. There are plenty of trailer kits that use bolts for assembly. If you haven't done much welding and don't have a welder, stick to a bolt-assembly kit. There isn't a significant difference in strength between a trailer that is bolted together and one that is welded.

In addition to assembly method, find out exactly what's included in the kit. This is one example of an ad for a trailer kit:

> "We offer the trailer axle(s), leaf springs, u-bolt kits, hanger kits, fenders, fender backs, light kits, wheels and tires mounted, jacks, couplers, wiring, and safety chains. You supply the steel, wood, and frame and the know how to complete your custom built trailer."

If you have to supply the trailer frame and deck this is a big deal. A trailer kit without a frame and trailer deck isn't much of a kit. Some companies, though, supply everything but the decking. That's going to be a lot easier to locate and haul home than lengths of structural steel.

Trailer kit prices vary greatly because they seldom include the same components. Read the fine print very carefully, and search out Internet forums where people relate their experiences with the different kits. You need to find a no-surprise kit.

Before you purchase your kit, look into the process for registering your trailer with the state. You will need to fill out a number of forms and likely have the trailer weighed. In some states, that's all that's necessary for trailers less than 1,000 pounds. In other states, you have to have the trailer inspected by a state employee. In some states, the license fee is based on how much you spent building your trailer, so you will need to retain your receipts. Check out the rules for your state before you begin construction.

Your state will assign a VIN to your trailer and issue you a license plate. In most cases it's a relatively easy process, but you need to investigate the process for licensing before you purchase your kit. Your state's regulations might help you make a decision about which trailer kit to purchase. You might even decide to not bother with a trailer kit if your state is especially difficult when it comes to registering home-made trailers.

REBUILDING THE USED TRAILER

Oftentimes, you can get a worn-out trailer for a really cheap price. Worn-out may simply mean that the tires are dry-rotted and the lights don't work. Neither of these items is too difficult or expensive to repair.

Whether or not to buy a used trailer depends in part on the size of the trailer. I would really hesitate to buy a beaten-up fifth-wheel RV trailer. There are simply too many components that can be bad, including plumbing and electrical systems. Plus, fifth-wheel and gooseneck trailers are too big to work on in the average suburban driveway.

Boat owners seem to come across used boat trailers easily. Almost every marina has a selection of old boat trailers for sale that can be acquired at really low prices. These used boat trailers are often cheaper than purchasing a trailer kit. They all need work, but isn't that the point?

UTILITY TRAILER REBUILD

A used utility trailer is my kind of trailer. It's cheap, it has very few moving parts, and it doesn't take up a lot of storage space.

All trailers have the same basic components; it's just the frame that might be different. Obviously, a boat-trailer frame is different from a utility trailer. Nonetheless, both have the following components: tires and wheels, bearings, lights, springs, and tie-downs. None of these items should cause you to reject a used trailer. Each component can be repaired or replaced, and a fair price depends on which items need repair or replacement. If you're new to the world of trailers, check out several websites to see what's available in the way of parts and get an idea of how much it will cost to rehabilitate this old trailer.

If you see a trailer that has a crack or bend in the main frame members, just walk away. A cracked trailer can be repaired, but it's seldom worth the cost and effort.

Tires

Tires may be the biggest deal when considering a used trailer. Check the condition of the sidewalls for cracking. Trailers seldom wear out the tread of a tire. Instead, trailer

continued on page 151

I purchased this trailer used for $500. I knew it needed some work, but it was a good deal nonetheless. My first order of business was to inspect the trailer to see exactly how much work would be required.

147

I always start by inspecting the wheel bearings. Removing the dust cap is the first step. This tool makes the job pretty easy, but no one appears to make this tool anymore. A big screwdriver and a hammer will do the job nearly as well. See Chapter 9 for more information about removing, inspecting, greasing, and replacing bearings.

Always make certain that the pin that goes through the receiver has some form of positive attachment. The clip shown here will retain the pin. You don't have to think a great deal about what would happen should this pin fall out of your receiver. It's not a bad idea to check on this pin as you walk around your trailer in the rest-stop area.

If you have a dual-axle trailer, check the condition of the equalizer. The one in this picture is brand new so it should be good. Make sure to look for cracks, though. You can never be too careful here.

The wiring system on this trailer is a mess. The only good thing here is that the white ground wire is securely attached. You have two choices for solving this problem. Just replace the whole mess, or spend twice as long trying to troubleshoot the system and fix the problems.

This is the way the trailer ball should look. The threads on the ball should actually extend beyond the nut on the bottom. If you can't tighten your trailer ball to look like this, start shopping for a new one.

Read the directions. My trailer is rated at 3,500 pounds, so it only made sense that the ball mount should be rated the same. Notice that this mount can be used in an up or down position. That means you have 4 1/2 inches of adjustment. That should cover most situations.

This is a D-ring tie-down. They're tough and they're inexpensive. You're going to have to cut a hole in your trailer deck to install them, but that's easy enough to do.

Unfortunately, this trailer came with car tires. Note the number 94T. The 94 is the load rating. That means I have a tire that can only carry 1,477 pounds. Multiply that by two and you have 2,954 pounds. So this means the trailer and whatever is loaded on it can't exceed 2,954 pounds.

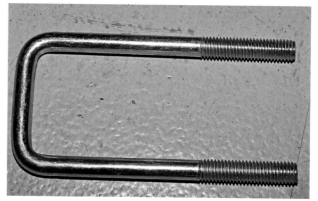

Be sure to check the U-bolts. You'll need to replace any cracked ones. Luckily, they come in standard sizes, so replacements are cheap and easy to find.

A little more time and a little more sandpaper and I found out that my trailer had a real serial number. Using the Florida computer system, I also discovered that the trailer was first registered in 1970.

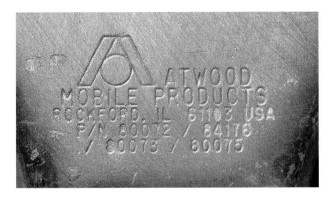

As you begin assessing your trailer, it pays to see where the parts came from. With the help of a little sandpaper, I was able to determine that my coupler came from Atwood Mobile Products, and that the part number was 80072. Then, with the help of Yahoo Search, I was able to figure out that I had a more than adequate A-frame coupler. Actually, it's rated at 5,000 pounds.

Next, I crawled under the trailer to inspect the springs. They had the usual surface rust, but nothing to be concerned about. All of the leaves were intact and everything was properly aligned.

continued from page 147

tires go bad from age, and the sidewall is the best indication of tire condition. In addition, check the size and brand of the tire. All the tires should be the same brand and size. You certainly don't want tires with two different diameters.

Wheels

To evaluate the wheels on a used trailer, first check to see if they're straight. I use a dial indicator, which is probably overkill. You can rig up a pointer to do almost the same thing. Bent wheels can be a problem because you usually can't replace just one. You have to have a matched set of wheels. This means a long search for an exact replacement or buying several wheels that match.

Next, check the lug nut seats. These seats can be damaged by overtightening the nut or improperly installing the wheel. If the lug nut seat is badly torn up, you'll have to buy a new wheel. Actually, you'll probably end up buying two new wheels since it's not easy to match an old trailer wheel.

Finally, check the thread on the lug nuts and wheel studs. I've seen more damaged wheel studs than lug nuts over the years. This damage is usually a result of overtightening. Another common lug nut problem is having several different types of lug nuts, requiring two or three sockets to remove two wheels from the trailer. You want to standardize your lug nut size before you have to remove a wheel in some sort of emergency. Once again, your local auto-parts store can come to your rescue.

Bearings

Bearings are pretty easy to check. First, check for noise. Jack up the trailer and listen for noise coming out of the hub area. Spin the wheel while it's off the ground. If you hear a noise or the wheels are hard to turn, you have bad bearings and you'll have to replace them.

Next, check for bearing play. If it's really bad, you'll actually be able to move the wheel back and forth. If you determine that you have excessive bearing play, try adjusting them first. It may be that the last owner didn't properly adjust them. You'll have to remove the cotter pin and use a crescent wrench to loosen and then tighten the large bearing

While you're still on the ground, check on the condition of the bearing seals. You'll know right away if you have a problem with a faulty grease seal because this area will be covered in grease—and not just a light coating of it, either.

nut. Remember to spin the wheel while tightening the spindle nut.

Lights

Lights are simple to check. If you find more than three splices, or if nothing works, just rip everything out and start over again. Installing a new wiring system is usually easier than spending hours trying to troubleshoot the old wiring system. Starting over also allows you to upgrade the lighting system and consider LED lights. The only practical difference between LED lights and conventional lighting is the price; the wiring is exactly the same. If you need to rewire the trailer, you may choose to add additional clearance or running lights to your trailer.

Springs

Springs break more often than they wear out. The true wear item on leaf springs is the bushing in the eye of the leaf spring. These bushings are readily available and easily replaced.

Here's a wiring trick that has suited me well over the years. I made this jumper wire several years ago as a tool for finding grounding problems. I attach one end to the tow truck's battery and run the wire back to the marker and taillights. If I clip onto the hot side of the light and still get no light I have a grounding problem. For less than $10 I've saved a lot of troubleshooting time over the years.

You'll find a wide price range when you're looking for trailer lighting kits. LED packages are quite expensive—over $100. The conventional lights pictured here cost $49.95.

A broken leaf in any of your springs means that you must buy new leaf springs. You shouldn't buy a new spring for just one side of your trailer; you need to balance out the trailer with new springs on both sides. Most trailer stores have a huge variety of leaf springs to choose from. I think it's best to remove one of the springs and take it to the local trailer store than it is to order springs online. Besides, the shipping costs might even be greater than the cost of the spring.

Tie-Downs

You're most likely going to replace the entire tie-down system on any used trailer you purchase. There's little point in trying to adapt the previous owner's system to your needs. You really need to determine if you can easily create a new system that meets your needs.

Evaluating and replacing tie-downs can be a little tricky. Do you only plan to haul one thing on your trailer, or are you going to put it to work hauling a variety of things? Trailer stores have a huge variety of different tie-downs. It's worth spending an hour looking at all of the possible choices that are available before you purchase your used trailer.

Your first priority in tie-downs is strength. Then, you need to decide on things like the ability to swivel or the ability to be stored flat with the trailer deck when not in use. You might even think about using an E-track system of tie downs. Take your time and look at all of the options.

GLOSSARY

ball height: This is the distance from the ground to the center of the hitch ball. This measurement is made when both the trailer and the tow vehicle are parked on a flat surface and parallel to the ground. You can use this measurement to determine the amount of drop or rise necessary for the trailer ride parallel to the ground when being towed.

ball mount: This is the removable hitch ball platform that slides into the receiver of a hitch. It's usually fastened in place with a pin and clip. There are a variety of different ball mounts available. This means the ball mount can be used to raise or lower the height of the ball to allow for level trailer towing. *See also draw bar.*

bolt-on hitch (a permanent undercar hitch): This type of hitch attaches directly to the tow vehicle and provides the connection between the tow vehicle and the trailer. A fixed-tongue hitch includes the ball platform as part of the hitch. A receiver-style hitch has a receptacle (usually 1 1/4 inches or 2 inches square) for inserting special ball mounts or bike racks. The receiver hitch allows for a lot more versatility.

brake controller: This is an electronic device that's mounted in the tow vehicle to control the trailer brakes. This controller is connected to the tow vehicle's brake system and it senses when the brakes need to be applied to the trailer. There's usually a lever to manually operate the trailer brakes.

breakaway switch: This is an electrical switch designed to engage the brakes in case the trailer breaks away from the tow vehicle. The switch is often mounted on the tongue of the trailer and connected by a very small cable to the tow vehicle.

bumpers: These are the parts on a vehicle that protect the front and rear ends in the event of an accident. In the old days they were made of steel and chrome plated. Today, they are all-plastic components. Some trucks and SUVs still have steel rear bumpers. By this I mean you can attach a small hitch ball to these bumpers for towing, but they're only safe for use with light-duty trailers.

chassis: This term is usually used to refer to the frame of a motorhome. It includes not only the frame but also the engine, transmission, drivetrain, axles, and wheels. When the term is used in reference to a van or truck, the chassis also includes the cab.

Class 1 (or Class I) hitch: This is a very-light-duty trailer hitch with a capacity of up to 2,000 pounds gross trailer weight and 200 pounds tongue weight.

Class 2 (or Class II) hitch: The first step up from the Class 1 trailer hitch has a weight-carrying rating of up to 3,500 pounds gross trailer weight and 300 to 350 pounds tongue weight.

Class 3 (or Class III) hitch: Class 3 trailer hitches have a weight-carrying capacity of up to 5,000 pounds of gross trailer weight and 500 pounds tongue weight. Sometimes used to refer to any hitch with a 2-inch receiver, regardless of rating.

Class 4 (or Class IV) hitch: A Class 4 trailer hitch usually carries a rating of 10,000 to 12,000 pounds gross trailer weight and 1,000 to 1,200 pounds tongue weight. Many times, any hitch with a capacity greater than 5,000 pounds gross weight is referred to as a Class 4 hitch. These are most often used for towing RV travel trailers.

Class 5 (or Class V) hitch: This hitch is designed for loads greater than 10,000 pounds and more than 200 pounds of tongue weight. This hitch usually has a 2 1/2-inch receiver box and uses a ball with a 2-inch diameter. A weight distribution system is essential with this large a load. These hitches are usually used with large car trailers, horse trailers, and large boat and camping trailers.

converter: This is a black box that converts three-wire tow vehicle electrical systems to two-wire systems by integrating the stop and turn-signal circuits that are common in trailer wiring. It's most often used with foreign cars and trucks, although it's becoming necessary on more domestic vehicles.

coupler: This is what the trailer ball attaches to. It's the most forward part of the trailer tongue that envelops and secures to the tow vehicle hitch ball. These couplers can be either welded or bolted into place on the trailer tongue.

curb weight: You might think of this as the weight of your truck as it's ready to drive down the road. It's the weight of a vehicle full of fuel and all fluids, but with no one in the car or truck. When we use the term curb weight with a trailer, it's the weight of the trailer, with all the equipment in place—full fuel tanks, full fresh water tanks, full propane bottles, and all other equipment fluids—but before taking on any passengers or personal cargo. Curb weight does not include passengers. It's only the weight of the vehicle or trailer.

custom hitch: This is used to describe a hitch that is designed for a particular year, make, and model of vehicle. *See also hitch, fixed-tongue hitch, bolt-on hitch, receiver-style hitch, and round-tube hitch.*

The coupler is bolted to the trailer tongue.

draw bar: A draw bar is a removable coupling platform that slides into the hitch receiver. It's then fastened into place with a pin and a clip, just like a normal trailer ball. Sometimes this term is used to distinguish a coupling configuration (such as a pintle hook) that's different from the standard ball mount we're all familiar with. *See also ball mount.*

equalizer: *See weight distribution system.*

fifth-wheel hitch: A Class 5 hitch that mounts in the bed of a pickup truck and uses a plate in the bed of the truck. This system is very similar to a semi-tractor trailer. The fifth-wheel is bolted in place directly above the rear axle. This means that several feet of the trailer hang over the tow vehicle. Normally, you can place about 15 to 25 percent of the trailer's weight on the rear axle of the truck. Commercial trucks and trailers use this hitch configuration. It's also very common with large horse trailers, race car haulers, and large RV trailers.

fixed-tongue hitch: This is a hitch with an integral ball platform that cannot be removed. The ball platform is usually welded in place. *See also custom hitch, hitch, bolt-on hitch, receiver-style hitch, and round-tube hitch.*

gooseneck: A Class 5 hitch that mounts on a ball in the bed of a pickup truck (either 2 5/16 inches or 3 inches in diameter) to engage a coupler on a trailer. This shouldn't be confused with a fifth-wheel hitch. The trailer is connected to the tow vehicle with a standard ball hitch in the truck bed. Often there's a vertical, slender arm on the front of the trailer. Gooseneck hitches are common on longer horse and utility trailers.

gooseneck adapter: This adapter allows you to attach a gooseneck trailer to a truck that has a fifth-wheel in place.

It couples with a ball hitch mounted in the bed of a truck, enabling the fifth-wheel to be towed like a gooseneck trailer. Quite simply, it's an adapter where one end attaches to the king pin on your fifth-wheel trailer, and the other end accepts the standard-size 2 5/16-inch gooseneck ball.

gross combined vehicle weight (GCVW): The total combined weight of your trailer and tow vehicle. This includes all passengers and everything you've loaded into the trailer and the tow vehicle.

gross trailer weight (GTW): This is the total weight of a trailer, including everything you've loaded into it, or on top of it. Gross trailer weight is the same as gross vehicle weigh when referring to a trailer.

gross vehicle weight (GVW): This is the total weight of a vehicle, including all of its contents and passengers. Gross vehicle weight is the actual weight of the fully loaded vehicle or trailer, including all cargo, fluids, passengers, and optional equipment. This is what your vehicle would weigh if you drove it onto a scale as you leave for a trip.

gross vehicle weight rating (GVWR): This is the weight specified by a manufacturer as the recommended maximum weight of a vehicle when fully loaded. You can only exceed this number at your own risk. If your car, truck, or trailer exceeds this rating, you have too much stuff.

hand wheel: Somewhat uncommon, this threaded wheel on the top of the trailer coupler tightens or loosens the coupler assembly around the hitch ball. Most trailers today use a locking lever, but the hand wheel is still around.

hardtop: A rigid metal or fiberglass structure that fastens to a vehicle and encloses the trailer. The most common application is on snowmobile trailers. The hard top lifts up for loading and is then lowered down to the deck of the trailer to keep road salt and slush off the snowmobiles.

hitch: A device that attaches directly to a tow vehicle to connect the tow vehicle and the trailer. Hitch installations are most often considered permanent. A fixed-tongue hitch includes a flat nonremovable draw bar, while a receiver-style hitch has a receptacle (typically 1 1/4 inches or 2 inches) for inserting special ball mounts or bike racks. *See also custom hitch, fixed-tongue hitch, permanent undercar hitch, receiver-style hitch, and round-tube hitch.*

hitch ball: The ball-shaped attachment to a hitch onto which a trailer coupler is attached. The largest variety of hitch balls is available at a specialized trailer store, but most people purchase them at the local auto-parts store.

hitch bar: *See ball mount or draw bar.*

hitch weight: *See tongue weight.*

insert: Any item that slides into a receiver-style hitch is called an insert. There are a huge variety of inserts available that allow you to attach everything from a bike rack to an electric winch. I won't even get into the decorative inserts such as the spinning propellers and illuminated skulls that are found on every road in the United States.

inverter: A device that converts direct current (DC) to alternating current (AC) in order to power AC equipment while the RV is not plugged into an AC source. These are usually found in RV trailers and race car haulers. The typical DC source is a battery, although solar panels are becoming more popular.

jackknife: This is what happens when the trailer tongue or body swings into contact with the tow vehicle. Jackknife accidents usually occur while backing up, although more creative folks have found unique, and equally damaging, ways of doing this.

king pin: The pin by which a fifth-wheel trailer attaches to the truck. It slides into the fifth-wheel hitch and locks in place.

king pin weight: The actual weight pressing down on the fifth-wheel hitch by the trailer is called king pin weight. It's the same concept as tongue weight. The recommended amount of king pin weight is 15 to 25 percent of the gross trailer weight. This is also sometimes called pin weight.

leveling jack: These jacks lower from the underside of trailers and motorhomes for the purpose of leveling the vehicle. A leveling jack is designed to bear a significant portion of the RV's weight. In some cases, you can even use a leveling jack to lift a trailer off the ground.

locking pin: A hitch pin that locks with a key to prevent theft of a ball mount or other insert.

lunette eye: This is the huge round metal ring used in place of a ball coupler on some commercial and agricultural trailers. It attaches to a pintle hook that's located on the towing vehicle.

payload: This is the weight of all the stuff you put into, or on top of, your trailer. Another description is that it's the weight of the trailer's load.

pin: Pins are used to fasten any insert (e.g., ball mount, bike rack) into a receiver hitch. They're available in both standard and locking configurations.

pintle hitch: A common heavy-duty coupling type that utilizes a pintle hook attached to a tow vehicle to pull a trailer with a lunette eye. Pintle hitches are commonly used on military, construction, industrial, and agricultural equipment.

pintle hook: This is the "jaw" portion of a pintle hitch that attaches to the tow vehicle.

pintle mount: This is a specialized insert for a receiver hitch. It's really a shank with a flat plate that allows you to bolt a pintle hook into place. These mounts are typically adjustable for vertical height.

plug: The connector used to connect trailer wiring to a tow vehicle. They come in varying levels of complexity depending on how many wires are required for your trailer.

receiver: This is the part of a trailer hitch that accommodates inserts such as ball mounts, draw bars, or accessory carriers. Common receiver sizes are 1 1/4 inches and 2 inches. Some of the smaller trucks and SUVs come with the smaller size in an effort to keep you from overloading the vehicle with a heavy trailer.

receiver cover: A temporary end cap that inserts into a 1 1/4-inch or 2-inch hitch receiver. It's designed to protect from the elements and also used to cover up the hitch when not in use. Some of them, such as the ones with the Harley Davidson logos, allow you to make a statement.

receiver-style hitch: Any hitch with a receptacle (typically 1 1/4 inches or 2 inches) that accommodates inserts such as draw bars, ball mounts, or bike racks. *See also custom hitch, fixed-tongue hitch, bolt-on hitch, hitch, and round-tube hitch.*

roll pan: A fascia panel used in place of a rear bumper, common on lowered trucks. Installation of a roll pan may interfere with placement of a bolt-on hitch. Actually, they make it almost impossible to install a hitch.

safety chains: Chains that are attached to the trailer tongue with hooks on their free ends. These chains keep the trailer connected to the tow vehicle should the coupler or hitch ball detach from the tow vehicle. Safety chains must be in place every time you tow. It's the law in 46 states.

spring bar: A key component in a weight-distributing hitch system. Spring bars work to distribute trailer tongue loads to the tow vehicle's forward axle.

stabilizing jack: These jacks are inserted under or lowered from trailers and motorhomes for the purpose of stabilizing the vehicle. A stabilizing jack isn't designed to bear a significant portion of the RV's weight but rather a small amount in order to reduce movement during occupancy. Stabilizing jacks are normally found toward the backs of trailers. Even some of the large slides on RV trailers use stabilizing jacks today.

surge brake system: A surge brake system is entirely self-contained on the trailer and is activated when the tow vehicle decelerates. The momentum of the trailer pushes the surge brake housing forward. This drives the pushrod connected to the coupler into the master cylinder. Brake fluid is then forced out of the master cylinder into the wheel cylinders or pistons that apply the trailer brakes. The entire activation process is completed in less than one second. Hydraulic surge brake systems can be used by a variety of tow vehicles and can accommodate a variety of trailer loading conditions without requiring any adjustment.

The chains are heavy enough for the trailer, and the hooks are more than sturdy enough.

sway control device: A device similar to a shock absorber that resists swaying movement of a trailer tongue sometimes caused by passing vehicles or wind.

tag-along trailer: Tag-along trailers, also called bumper pull trailers, attach to a hitch on the hauling vehicle. The trailer tags along behind the tow vehicle and doesn't become a part of the overall vehicle.

tandem axle: Two axles (four wheels).

tongue: The part of the trailer that extends forward from the trailer box and includes the coupler.

tongue weight (TW): This is the weight applied by the trailer on the hitch ball. Generally, tongue weight should not be more than 15 percent of the gross trailer weight. *See also weight distribution system.*

tow bars: These are attached to the front of a vehicle, allowing it to be towed by another vehicle while riding on its own wheels. This is mostly used by people who have motorhomes and need a small car once they get to their RV site.

tow vehicle (towing vehicle): The vehicle that pulls a trailer.

toy hauler: The term "toy hauler" is applied to both fifth-wheels and travel trailers, and it describes an RV designed to carry toys—small cars, dune buggies, four wheelers, motorcycles, and so on. The distinguishing feature of a toy hauler is the large door in the back of the trailer, which opens down, creating a ramp for getting the toys out of the trailer.

travel trailer: A towable trailer that hitches onto a ball mount on the tow vehicle and is designed as living quarters for recreational travel.

unloaded vehicle weight (UVW): This is the weight of a vehicle as it leaves the factory. It includes full engine and generator fuel tanks and fluids. It doesn't include cargo, water, propane, or dealer-installed accessories. It may or may not include factory-installed options. Some manufacturers weigh each unit to determine UVW, while others provide only the average or estimated weight for each model.

Volt-Ohmmeter (VOM): Also called a multimeter, the Volt-Ohmmeter is a very handy tool for troubleshooting electrical systems. It can be used to test cables, AC power levels, and batteries. A digital Volt-Ohmmeter lets you measure voltage and current easily.

weight-carrying hitch: Any hitch used without a weight-distributing system is considered a weight-carrying hitch. Some hitches are designed and clearly marked "weight-carrying only." Some hitches are weight-carrying with weight-distributing ability and will have a dual rating.

weight-distributing hitch: A ball hitch system that distributes some of the tongue weight to all axles of the tow vehicle and trailer. With standard ball hitches, all of the tongue weight rests on the tow vehicle's rear axle; the weight-distributing hitch uses spring bars to distribute this weight among the axles. This system puts more weight on the front axle for better steering control and less weight on the rear axle to allow towing a heavier trailer that may otherwise overload the rear axle.

weight distribution system: This type of hitch system is built around a receiver hitch that includes supplemental equipment, such as spring bars that work to distribute trailer tongue loads to the trailer axle(s) and the tow vehicle front axle. A weight distribution system greatly enhances handling and braking and at the same time increases trailer-towing capacity beyond what's recommended when a weight-carrying hitch is used.

APPENDIX:
BASIC TRAILER TIPS

TIRES AND WHEELS

- Always use the proper torque setting for wheel nuts. This is usually specified by the wheel or trailer manufacturer. Too much torque can permanently damage the wheel, while not enough torque can result in stud failure, or a wheel coming off.
- Check lug nut torque frequently. Each time a wheel is removed and remounted, the lug nuts should be checked and retightened after 50 miles, 150 miles, 300 miles, and periodically thereafter.
- Wheels and tires must always be matched to ensure safe, reliable performance. It's best that all the tires be the same size and from the same manufacturer.
- If you're using aftermarket wheels, make sure they fit properly and the wheel studs are long enough to allow proper thread engagement. When you tighten the lug nuts, some threads from the stud should be showing.
- Always make sure the tires on your trailer are inflated to the proper air pressure as specified by the trailer manufacturer. If you have any questions, check with your local trailer store.
- Make sure there's enough clearance around the sides and top of the tires to prevent the tires from rubbing on the frame or other trailer structure.
- If you have uneven tire wear, it's important to note the type and nature of the wear pattern in order to determine the cause. Contact your local trailer store for troubleshooting the problem.
- While it's not common for a wheel to leak air, don't try to solve the problem by putting a tube in the tire. The only safe solution for a leaky wheel is to replace it.

BEARINGS

- Always inspect and service the wheel bearings according to your owner's manual. If you don't have an owner's manual, contact the trailer manufacturer to see if one is still available. Your local trailer store might be able to help out if you can't determine who built your trailer.
- Your owner's manual should outline the proper bearing adjustment method. You can also use the procedures outlined in Chapter 9.

BRAKES

- Remember to lubricate the moving parts in your brakes according to the manufacturer's recommendations. Proper maintenance here will prevent these parts from seizing up during storage. Only use grease that's designated for use on brake parts. Don't use chassis or bearing grease around your braking system.
- Inspect your emergency breakaway device periodically to make sure it's in good working order.
- Replace brake shoes, or pads, if the linings have been contaminated with oil or grease. Also replace them if the linings are less than 1/16 inch thick or are abnormally scored or gouged. Minor cracks in linings are not a problem unless pieces of the linings are missing.
- Remember that your new brake shoes need to be broken in. The lining material needs some time to match the surface of the brake drum or disc. This means that when you install new brakes, they won't be as effective as the old brakes you just replaced. This process may take quite a few stops to get the shoes fully worn in before maximum brake performance can be achieved. Be careful for the first few hundred miles of use, and avoid rapid stops. Give the new brake material time to conform to the drums or discs.

HITCHES

- Always tow your trailer so that it's running level. If the hitch is too high or too low, the trailer axle(s) will be unevenly loaded and can result in premature tire or axle failure.
- When loading your trailer, make sure enough weight is being carried on the hitch to allow proper weight distribution and good handling.

LOAD DISTRIBUTION

- Don't exceed the capacity of your trailer. Overloading your trailer will seriously shorten the life of the various components. It can also result in unsafe braking.
- The location of the load on a trailer will affect the ride characteristics. Too little load on the hitch can cause the trailer to wander or sway. Too much load on the hitch can overload your tow vehicle's suspension.
- Remember that the gross axle weight rating (GAWR) of your running gear is determined by the lowest-rated component in the assembly.
- Always support the back of the trailer at the ramps when loading equipment or vehicles to prevent overloading the rear axle.

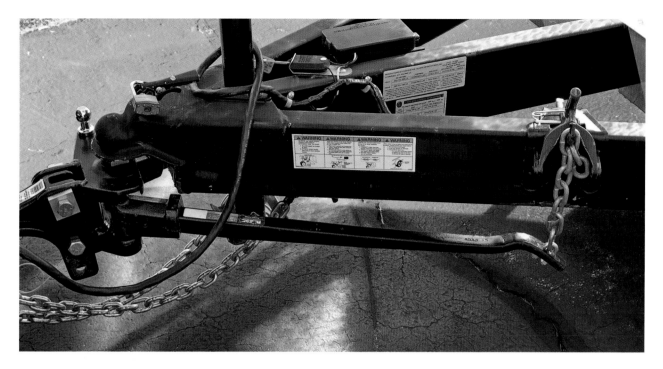

If you're towing a big trailer, a load equalizer is very important. When you adjust the bar, you place more weight on the front wheels of the tow vehicle, enabling the tow vehicle and the trailer to ride parallel to the ground.

Notice how far back the axles are on this trailer.

AXLES

- Axles should be spaced far enough apart to allow a minimum of 1 inch clearance between the tires. More space would be required if tire chains are to be used.
- The widest possible track and axle mounting provides the best design for stability.
- Bump clearance is the distance from the top of a leaf spring–mounted axle to the bottom of the frame. If this distance is too small, the axle can come in contact with the frame and result in damage to the axle.

INDEX